TRAPATTONI

A LIFE IN FOOTBALL

EGON THEINER AND
ELISABETH SCHLAMMERL

LIB
ERT
IES

CONTENTS

FOREWORD

'*Il vecchio Trap*' – good old Trapattoni. Ireland's new football manager is not so much a highly experienced, much-decorated coach as a much-loved national institution. Think of old Bill Shankly, throw in a little Bill Nicholson, and top it off with a dollop of Jack Charlton, and you have him.

The big difference, of course, is that whereas the two Bills, Shankly and Nicholson, have long since shuffled off this mortal coil, '*il vecchio Trap*' is still at it, winning league titles across half of Europe. Will he now be able to work his magic for Ireland or, at sixty-nine years of age, has the time come even for him when he should be thinking of his slippers, the fireside and the TV?

Those who feel that Trapattoni's appointment as Irish manager might represent a job too far for this much-travelled coach might do well to pause for thought. It is true that he comes from an older generation, from a time when good manners, saying the rosary and putting dobbin on your boots held serious sway. There is nothing wrong with that. Yet he also grew up in a hard school, one which nurtured his competitive instincts:

I had a hard and difficult childhood. At three years of age, I had diphtheria. There was never much money around. But now I would say that precisely that hard and poor childhood was my good fortune and in a sense is the key to my life. It helped me understand the meaning and the significance of so many things and to distinguish the true from the futile.

Those words, spoken in an interview back in 1989, are as true today as they were then. 'Trap' grew up tough and rough, and made his own way up the greasy pole of football success.

Born in a modest dwelling in the Milan industrial hinterland of Cusano Milanino, Trap was the fifth of five, the spoiled baby of the family. He was born at home on 17 March 1939 (St Patrick's Day – a good omen surely) in a small tenement building, now destroyed but then inhabited by no less than sixteen families.

His father, Francesco, a peasant farmer from Barbata near Bergamo, in the foothills of the Alps, had moved to Cusano Milanino in search of work. Francesco found a job at the Gerli factory, a textile company that produced rayon, a type of silk. Francesco would work a fourteen-hour shift and then go straight from the factory floor to work with nearby farmers, cutting grass, feeding livestock or mending fences.

Francesco rarely had time to come home between the factory and the farm, so young Giovanni would be sent out with a bag of sandwiches for him:

I would stay there and watch him eat the sandwiches. He would finish them in a minute: he ate so fast
because he didn't want to be wasting time.

Trap grew up in wartime. Some of his earliest memories are of being lifted, half-asleep, out of his bed and
rushed to a shelter as the air-raid sirens blazed and the
Allied bombs fell. He even became friendly with some of
the German soldiers who manned an anti-aircraft gun
that had been set up in his courtyard.

His earliest football memories, too, recall those days
of hardship. He learned to play football on the street,
kicking around a stuffed pig's bladder. ('None of us ever
had a real ball.') He began his team football with the San
Martino 'Oratorio', the local parish youth team, where he
was spotted by Antonio Crippa, a local talent scout linked
to AC Milan.

When the time came for him to have a trial with the
big Milan club, his father almost scuppered the deal. A
friend had offered Francesco a job in the bank for young
Giovanni. To Francesco, that looked a much safer bet.
However, 'Il Guan' (as he was known) and the talent
scout stuck to their guns, giving rise to a career that saw
him play 284 games in Serie A (mainly for AC Milan) as
well as seventeen times for Italy.

Trap played alongside some legendary figures. He was
the midfield wood-cutter and water-fetcher for 'golden
boy' Gianni Rivera, and he was often back there in
defence helping out captain Cesare Maldini, father of the
peerless Paolo Maldini. Critics of the time recall Trap not

only as a dour, battling midfielder but also as a key weapon in the Milan armoury.

For example, when Milan won the 1963 Champions Cup at Wembley, beating Benfica 2–1, Trap played a key role. Benfica had started that game well, with their great striker Eusébio opening the scoring. Frustrated by the way Eusébio seemed to be running the game, Milan coach Nereo Rocca switched the marking, putting Trap on the Portuguese ace. From then on, the music changed. Eusébio, under fierce marking, faded from the game and Milan came back to win 2–1.

Nor was Eusébio the only famous scalp to fall Trap's way. A generation of Italian fans recall how he marked the great Pelé right out of an Italy v. Brazil friendly in May 1963. One fierce Trap tackle early in the game and Pelé was gone. These days, Trap plays it down, saying that Pelé was not fit that day . . . but the legend lives on.

If 'Il Trap' was much respected as a player, as a coach he has become nothing less than a 'living legend'. His thirty-five-year-long coaching record is so full of league titles (seven in Italy, one in Germany, one in Portugal, one in Austria) and various Cups (including the Champions, UEFA and Intercontinental Cups) that it fills half a page of that Italian bible, the *Annuario Del Calcio Mondiale*. At club level, he has won it all. What is more, be it Juventus, AC Milan, Inter Milan, Bayern Munich, Fiorentina, Benfica or, as most recently, Red Bull Salzburg, he always gets the team to play for him.

Yet here we come to a bone of contention. Just what sort of football do they play for him? For many years now, many fans and commentators alike have looked on Trapattoni as nothing less than the high priest of *catenaccio*. He is not the first – nor will he be the last – Italian coach to send out a team that knows how to defend, but when it comes to 'copper-fastening' the result, no one does it better than Trap.

It was in this context then that, just after he had been appointed Italy coach in July 2000, the sports daily *Gazzetta Dello Sport* asked him a leading question. Which do you prefer: getting the result or playing well? It was not quite an 'Are-you-still-beating-the-wife?' question, but it was close. Trap's not-unexpected answer was revealing:

> I remember (coach) Fulvio Bernardini's Bologna team (1961–65). For two years, people went around saying that a side can play that well only in heaven. But they didn't win anything. In the third season, they didn't play nearly so well, but they won the title. . . . If you play badly but you get a result, you have to thank God. The result is very important.

As someone who grew up under the tutelage of AC Milan coach Nereo Rocco, Trap has always been portrayed as a flag-bearer for the *catenaccio* way. Rocco practised a very defensive game and furthermore was famous for sayings such as: 'Let's hope it's a good game but that the better team doesn't win.'

Back in 1989, the season in which Trap won the Serie A title with Inter Milan, the late Gianni Brera, an outstanding football writer of his day, was asked about Trap. Was he really the inheritor of the Rocco tradition?

'Of course,' Brera responded. 'And he is so in relation to a pretty fundamental rule, namely that when you build a house, you start with the foundations not the roof. Rocco and then Trapattoni have always built their sides on the basis of the principle that it is easier to concede one goal less than your opponents than to score one goal more than your opponents. It seems to me perfectly logical reasoning.'

Many of the great players to have been coached by Trapattoni have had reason to argue with this 'perfectly logical reasoning'. Trap himself recalls constant tactical disagreements with the current UEFA president, and one-time Juventus star, Frenchman Michel Platini:

> There was nobody like Michel. He was always shouting at me: 'Move forward, get up the field, the defence is too deep.' I would reply: 'OK, but first let's get on the ball.' I was always telling him that old story about the soldier who jumped out of his trench and got right in behind enemy lines. 'Captain, captain, I've taken thirty prisoners,' he reported. 'Oh yeah?' 'I swear it, captain.' 'I believe you, but first let me see the prisoners,' answered the captain.

Time has passed, and many players have come and gone. Trap has travelled from Munich to Salzburg via Lisbon, but the basic Trapattoni principles have changed little. The whole word saw those tenets in action at the 2002 World Cup and the 2004 European Championships.

In two key games, against South Korea and against Sweden, with the score 1–0 for Italy, he opted to 'copperfasten' the result in true Italian style, taking off strikers and tightening up his midfield. It was the sort of move that a thousand Italian coaches make every Sunday afternoon. It looked like Brera's 'perfectly logical reasoning'. Except that it backfired in both cases.

In 2002, South Korea battled away, first scoring an 87th-minute equaliser and then eliminating Italy with a 116th-minute golden goal from Ahn Jung Hwan. Against Sweden in Euro 2004, it was Zlatan Ibrahimovic who did the damage, with an 85th-minute equaliser for Sweden that left Italy with the draw that eventually saw them eliminated.

So, does all this mean that Trap is simply a hopelessly dour, defensive coach? Not so fast. Those of us old enough (and lucky enough) to have seen his Juventus side of the 1980s would beg to differ. That team often featured strikers Roberto Bettega and Paolo Rossi, flanked by ultra-attacking midfielders Platini and the Pole Zibi Boniek, or indeed his current 'assistant' within the Irish camp, Liam Brady. Defensive they were not. This was a side that played superb football and did so with utter conviction.

Likewise, even Trap's Italy, the side which brought most criticism down on his head, still played good football. If dame fortune did not necessarily smile on Trap in South Korea, many observers felt that the first hour of the 1–1 draw with Sweden in Portugal witnessed the best hour of football in the entire tournament.

On the many occasions that he has been accused of playing too defensive a game, Trap has often replied by pointing out that his sides nearly always feature three men up front. Look at the statistics, he will say. Six times between 1981 and 1989, sides coached by him topped the goal-scoring chart in Serie A:

> My ideal lineout is a 3–5–2 in which one of the mid-fielders is really an inside forward, so it would be 3–4–1–2.

It does not sound like such defensive stuff, does it? In reality, Trap is a quintessential pragmatist, someone who fashions his game around the talent available to him. Of course, that reflection in itself prompts a question about Trapattoni as Irish manager. It was one thing to practise a tight, containing possession game with the likes of Zoff, Cabrini, Scirea, Gentile, Tardelli, Furino, Boniek, Bettega and Platini or Brady; it may be quite another to do so with the current Irish squad.

When analysing 'Il Trap', it is worth remembering that along with the current England manager, Fabio Capello, he forms part of a very restricted elite. He is someone who has worked only with big-time clubs (and one big-time country, Italy). In his first twenty-one years as a coach, he worked with only four clubs: AC Milan, Juventus, Inter Milan, Juventus again, and then Bayern Munich. In other words, for much of his career as a coach, Trapattoni has been working with the very best around. Even the most enthusiastic Irish supporter, how-ever, would hesitate before suggesting that the current Irish squad contains many of the 'best around'.

Yet it may be worth recalling Trap's experiences when he first moved out of Italian football in the mid-1990s. His first season with Bayern Munich (1994–95) was far from a success, and Trap went back to Italy dissatisfied with himself, with Bayern having finished sixth in the Bundesliga. He felt that he had seriously under-achieved, partly because of his lack of good German:

> I told [club boss] Franz Beckenbauer that I feel I am only giving 50 percent of myself because my great strength is to dialogue with players, but here I cannot manage that as I would like.

Being Trap, of course, he did not leave it there. Rather, he returned to triumph with Bayern two years later, with his command of German much improved in the meantime. This would suggest that whatever initial problems he encounters with Ireland, linguistic or otherwise, '*il vecchio Trap*' will not let things rest there.

Then, too, Trapattoni has already put together a formidable back-room team with Ireland, turning to men like Liam Brady and Marco Tardelli. This comes as no surprise, since he has long shown loyalty to friends and players who 'do the business' for him.

Some years ago, this correspondent was commissioned to interview him for TV. To my surprise, I was instructed to get myself and the crew up to a place called Cinisello Balsamo, an industrial hinterland of Milan, which apparently, was 'Il Trap's private hideaway.

We had the precise address, but a typical Milanese March downpour made it just about impossible to recognise the car in front, let alone street signs that would lead us to Trapattoni. As we drove up and down the ugly, nondescript back streets of industrialised Greater Milan, we became convinced we had got it wrong.

Eventually, we pulled in at what looked like the correct address. Shurely shome mistake. We had pulled up in front of a busy garage, where some expensive-looking Mercedes and BMWs were up on jacks, having their toenails polished.

Ah well, we thought, at least the people in the garage will be able to direct us onto the right road. In we walk, and head for the little office, complete with hatch window, in the corner. Excuse me, I'm looking for . . . and there he was, behind the hatch window, Giovanni Trapattoni in person, smiling broadly, and patiently waiting for the foreign journalist.

So what was a living legend of Italian football doing sitting in the office of an obviously busy, upmarket garage, minding his own business, as mechanics stepped in and out to consult the foreman? The garage in question is owned by Pasquale Piccolo, a buddy with whom Trapattoni once formed a business partnership and with whom he has retained a lifelong friendship, still keeping his own private office there above the workshop. (During the subsequent World Cup, when his handling of the Italian team brought fierce criticism on his head, 'Il Trap' was regularly on the phone to Pasquale, checking out both what the papers were saying and the national mood.)

Before we sat down to do our interview, Trapattoni showed us round his own trophy room and then insisted on ordering coffee and biscuits for us. His old-fashioned good manners, his easy-going attitude (he did not seem much upset by the fact that we had arrived late for the interview) and his obvious warmth struck a strong contrast with picture of the tough, often much-agitated coach who had stumped up and down the most famous touchlines of Italy, aiming his ear-piercing, two-fingered whistle of warning at players such as Brady and Platini. Put simply, Trapattoni remains faithful to himself and his Cusano Milanino background.

At the subsequent 2002 World Cup, he delighted some and scandalised others by carrying a little bottle of Holy Water with him as he sat on the Italy bench. Trap often has that effect on his compatriots. His oftentimes colourful – not to say incomprehensible – way with words has regularly provoked no small amount of patient amusement.

He is famous for a saying that has passed into the Italian language: 'Non dire gatto finché non ce l'hai nel sacco' ('Don't say cat until you have it in the bag'). Which cat and which bag, remains to be seen, but perhaps this is merely a Cusano Milanino version of: 'Don't count your chickens until they have hatched.'

And how many Irish chickens will 'Trap L'Irlandese' manage to hatch? Perhaps more than some expect. After all, Trapattoni is more than just a professional, he is a football obsessive, one who has never been frightened of hard work. (In his book, The Italian Job, Gianluca Vialli, another big name to have been coached by Trapattoni, points out that from the age of fourteen to eighteen, Trap used to wake up at 3 AM to go to work in a bakery.)

Trapattoni is famous for saying that a good manager can improve a team by 5 percent while a bad manager can make it play 30 percent below its potential. Our suspicion is that, sooner or later, Ireland will start to show the effects of that 5 percent (or more) improvement. One thing is for sure: Trap will give it his best shot.

Talking to him on the eve of the 2002 World Cup, I was curious about how he saw his immediate future. His answer says a lot about the man, then and now:

> I've always thought of the future as a great opportunity. If you're frightened, you'll never know it; if you're weak, you'll never get there; but if you have hope, it will be another great chance for you.

PADDY AGNEW, Rome correspondent of the *Irish Times*, has covered Italian football extensively for TV, radio and the printed press since moving to Italy in 1985. He is the author of *Forza Italia: A Journey in Search of Italy and Its Football*.

OUT OF THE SUBURBS

CUSANO MILANINO
1939–1959

It was a hard time. The fascists were in power, World War II had just begun, and the people who lived in the country had things even tougher than those who lived in the city. The person who was to become one of the greatest football trainers of the modern era came into the world on the seventeenth of March 1939. He was born at 12.45 AM at his parents' home on Via 24 Maggio in a small village just outside Milan. The village has two parts to its name – for two areas that couldn't be more different from each other.

For Cusano Milanino should actually have been called Cusano e Milanino, or 'Cusano and Milanino'. The village is split in two by a road. On the one side is the historical part, dominated by workers and farming; it was originally called Cusano sul Seveso. At this time, there was no Milanino, but rather acres of fields. At the beginning of the twentieth century, the architect Luigi Buffoli attempted to create a Milan that was embedded in nature for the beautiful and the rich, watched over by eagles and other birds: Milanino. Builders, workers and upper-class citizens joined forces in order to cooperate on local issues.

Giovanni Trapattoni, as you may have already guessed, comes from Cusano. He is the son of Francesco and Romilda Bassani, who came from Barbata, a small town in the Bergamo province, close to Milan. They came to Cusano looking for work, and Francesco ended up in the Gerli wool-dying factory. He worked two shifts there and also did farm work in the fields: his workday was fourteen hours long. Romilda was a housewife. Giovanni Luciano Giuseppe was the youngest of five children. His elder siblings are Antonio, Maria (who would enter the convent as Sister Romilda at the age of nineteen), Elisabetta and Angela.

The young Giovanni weighed only six and a half pounds at birth and was given his paternal grandfather's name. He grew up in a poor home but was well looked after and was spoiled by the four women of the household. Giovanni had sky-blue eyes and blond curly hair, like a little angel; in fact, he had the same smiling eyes and mouth as those cupids you see in frescos and paintings. He cried his eyes out only once: when his hair was cut. He was six years old the first time he kicked a ball.

There were soon other reasons for tears. Milan was bombed during the war and there were continuous air-raid alarms. Each time the alarm sounded, the Trapattonis rushed to the nearest air-raid shelter, which was three hundred metres away from their house. Three hundred metres to survival. Three hundred metres: about three times the length of a football field. Nevertheless, the young Giovanni also found some interesting aspects to the war. The Bresso military airport was located close to Cusano and was guarded by the anti-aircraft defence servicemen. One of their positions was within walking distance of his parents' house, in a barracks with two missiles aimed at nothing, and five Germans. One of them was called Rudi, and Giovanni learnt his first German word from him: *tschüss,* or 'bye'. Hitler's military personnel were still supplied with chocolate, and the naive preschooler found the Germans to be quite friendly.

His father Francesco had given him a small wooden truck as a present, and the child thus became both a worker and an architect. A second toy was a pigskin, filled with straw and other materials. It didn't roll, but it was soft and light enough to serve as a ball. This was how the times of the street-ball battles began. Giovanni (who was the first in the family to dare to call his parents by the informal 'you' in Italian, instead of the formal terms used by children at that time) found great pleasure in sports and was able to show how well his legs and that piece of pigskin worked together.

Francesco was not happy when he noticed how much in love his son was with the ball, however. He admonished Giovanni to concentrate on school and on the important things in life. (Giovanni's elder brother Antonio had already been forbidden from spending too much time playing football.) He told Giovanni that you could only get ahead in life through schooling, not through sports. And he told his son that he had been given all the basics in life in order to succeed: an outfit for winter, one for summer, and one for the holidays. '*Ma che vita è questa?*' ('But what kind of life is this?') he asked. It was for the good of his future, his health and his work as a paid employee, his father told him.

Nonetheless, Giovanni Trapattoni's sports career continued – which was to be expected during the post-war years, when there was no television, and certainly no computer games. One of the few and best-loved diversions was the football that was played on the San Martino parish's pitch after dinner. The pitch was small, of course, but it was floodlit. Trapattoni and his friends let off steam here, giving themselves the names of famous players. They played for hours – until midnight, or even later, as long as the priest didn't turn off the electricity. The games were seven-against-seven: each team had a goalkeeper, three defenders, two midfielder and a striker. By the time they were on their way home, their football shirts were drenched in sweat, their knees were bruised and their was breathing heavy. It wasn't long before the working-class children began to challenge their peers from the other side of the street, and promised themselves: '*Figli di papa!*' ('We'll show those rich good-for-nothings!') Both teams definitely gave their all.

Most importantly, Giovanni Trapattoni got to know Gilberto Noletti, with whom he would later transfer to AC Milan. However, AC was not Giovanni's first love, but rather Juventus. After all, Antonio was a fan of that team. The first players that influenced Giovanni were Giampiero Boniperti, a Juventus striker, and Alfredo di Stefano. When the World Cup was broadcast in 1954, the fifteen-year-old Giovanni fell in love with the

Uruguayan-Italian Juan 'Pepe' Schiaffino's playing style: his vision of the game, tactical intelligence, and under-standing of how goals could be scored.

Giovanni Trapattoni cut his time in school short due to financial necessity. Although he was completely competent in his studies and would have been capable of attending grammar school, he had had enough of formal education after his third year in secondary school, and decided to enter the working world. He had already contributed some money here and there to the household by working during the summer holidays. He worked once, for instance, polishing furniture. Now, however, after having received the secondary-school diploma, he was taken on as a typographer at 'Riboldi', making 8,000 lire per month. But his heart belonged to the round leather ball, and his time working at the printer would be only temporary.

Trapattoni played for Frassati and it was there that he met Sandro Salvadore, with whom he would work in Milan. From Frassati, he was directed to the 'Unione Sportiva Cusano Milanino' by the Crippa brothers, the leaders of the sports club. (Cusano Milanino, incidentally, came out of the dressing room in a dark-blue strip – the colours of the Serie A club Inter Milan.) The young man soon became known for his propensity for running and the fact that he didn't shy away from slide tackling – although he didn't need this technique most of the time. He had what so many others lack: an understanding of the art of anticipation.

In 1956, at the age of seventeen, he was discovered by Mario Malatesta, the AC Milan youth coach. He was picked up in front of the event centre together with Gilberto Noletti. Cusano Milanino received a transfer fee of 600,000 lire for both players. Trapattoni's first test in the AC Milan strip was held on the Redaelli Square in Rogoredo, but the defender was soon playing in the San Siro, in AC Milan's junior team. It was then that his success began. In 1957, AC Milan won the Italian junior championship, beating AS Roma 2–0 in the final. A year later, he was once again victorious, this time in Rome, where the Milan team turned a halftime score of 0–1 into a 2–1 victory.

On 29 June 1958, in Stockholm, a seventeen-year-old football player with the nickname Pelé would become a world champion in Stockholm with the Brazilian team, thanks to a 5–2 win against their Swedish hosts. On the same day, an eighteen-year-old hopeful made his debut in the professional AC Milan team. Giovanni Trapattoni was put out against Como for the Italian Cup, and his team won 4–1, thanks to three goals by Carletto Galli. It was an anonymous entry to the first team for Trapattoni, however. In fact, he was worried that he would play badly, and preferred not to tell anybody about his upcoming performance. However, he had not reckoned with the media. The *Gazzetta dello Sport* wrote about the outstanding achievement of the various players, and named 'Trappattoni (Milan)' (with two 'p's) among them.

His father Francesco learnt about his son's successful debut from the newspaper. He commented somewhat bitterly (and perhaps with a hint of what was to come): 'So I'll never be able to see you play.' Three days later, Signor Francesco Trapattoni died of a heart attack. The attack came out of the blue: he had no previous known heart problems.

Among the various things that the father bequeathed to his son was his two-fingered way of whistling. Trapattoni uses this whistle every time he walks on to one of the world's great football fields. It's a whistle that was used by his father to get his children into order, to call them back home, and to end abruptly the football games which would have otherwise gone on for much too long. It is a whistle that you couldn't argue with. Even the young Trapattoni would have liked to be able to whistle like the older Francesco. That's how the most-recognised whistle used by a football coach came to be; some say it is the most famous Italian whistle. With just his two smallest fingers in the corners of his mouth, Trapattoni is able to get up to a very high frequency indeed. The Milan coach whistles an average of fifteen times during a game, but it can at times be twice that many, and it seems that you can hear a little of his father Francesco in every one of them.

ON THE FOOTBALL PITCH

AC MILAN AND VARESE
1959–1972

His first game playing in AC Milan's professional team, his upbringing, the sudden death of his father, and his mother's insecure future combined to have a psychologically overwhelming effect on Giovanni Trapattoni. He was tormented by pain and feelings of guilt. He wanted to stop playing football, get a job and take care of his mother. He earned less as a football player than he could as a typist. He went to Professor Bottani, AC Milan's psych-ologist, for advice. However, it was the telephone conversation that coach Giuseppe 'Gipo' Viani had with Giovanni's older brother that helped him make his decision. 'He would be well advised to keep on playing. He will earn enough to be able to take care of his mother.' Trapattoni remained a footballer and is, to this day, thankful to Viani: the club gave him a raise from 35,000 lire to 60,000 lire, and later to 100,000 lire.

Trapattoni is a man with character. He overcame this period of personal difficulties, threw himself into his work, and won the 1959 and 1969 Viareggio youth tournaments with AC Milan. This tournament is one of the most famous stages for junior teams worldwide. On 24 January 1960, Trapattoni played for the first time in a Serie A championship game – in Ferrara, against SPAL – as the right-back. Milan coach Luigi Bonizzoni decided just before the game to exchange Trapattoni for Alfio Giuseppe Fontana due to the bad ground conditions and Fontana's previous injuries. Unfortunately, the replacement was not in the best of condition himself. He was suffering a thirty-eight-degree-Celsius fever but didn't let anyone know about it. Nevertheless, he did his duty, and marked Egidio Morbello. AC Milan won 3–0, with two goals by José Altafini and a converted penalty by Nils Liedholm. Trappattoni also received hymns of praise. It would be a while before he lost the added, superfluous and incorrect 'P' in his name, but he was definitely set on making a name for himself.

After his Serie A debut, he bought a classical record as a present for himself. Trapattoni had always been musically inclined; he had been in the Cusano Milanino choir. As a player, Trapattoni was fluent, dynamic and aggressive. He read the game, without wanting to be the central focus. Others wore the number-ten shirt; others directed the play. His job was to keep the right flank quiet and in good order and to deal with opposition attacks. It was other people's job to make goals, but the headlines belonged to him when journalists reported on how he didn't allow an opponent a chance to play freely, or how he got the ball away from some big-name player. He was certainly aware of the respect that both his fellow club members and his opponents had for him. Karl-Heinz Schnellinger (Milan, 1965–1974) described his teammate as a footballer with eyes and elegance who didn't have to kick his opponents down. Helmut Haller (AC Bologna, 1962–68; Juventus, 1968–73) learnt first-hand how agreeable an opponent Trapattoni was: an opponent who was fair and didn't feel the need to kick the other player's legs out from under him.

Nevertheless, Giovanni Trapattoni's career did not continue in a linear fashion. In 1960, he was called up to play in the Italian Olympic team, to be trained by 'Gipo' Viani and Nereo Rocco. He became friends with Gianni Rivera, played with Tarcisio Burgnich and Giacomo Bulgarelli, and with Mario Trebbi, Sandro Salvadore and Giorgio Ferrini. The twenty-one-year-old, maybe still a little green, was shocked to realise that Rocco was drinking his Grignolino wine out of a Coca-cola bottle, despite the fact that alcoholic drinks were forbidden in the Olympic village. As far as the football was concerned, it was all proceeding perfectly, with a 3–1 win against Brazil, in which Gerson De Oliveira Nunes also played. With that win, the Olympic hosts qualified for the semi-finals against Yugoslavia. They tied 1–1 and unfortunately, they were eliminated on the toss of a coin. Since Italy also lost the third-place play-off against Hungary 1–2, Trapattoni failed to win any medal at all, never mind the gold.

The man from Milan found the love of his life during those days in Rome. As he left the training camp in Hotel Traiano with Giacomo Bulgarelli in order to indulge in a couple of glasses of sweet wine, he saw a young woman feeding animals. He stood stock-still, as though he had been hit by a bolt of lightning, and said: 'Giacomo, she is gorgeous.' The practical Bulgarelli answered: 'Giovanni, you have to tell *her* that, not me.' But Trapattoni's heart was pounding and his knees were shaking, so Luciano Magistrelli, the defender's roommate, took the initiative and went to talk to the young woman. 'Could you please do me a favour and talk to the blond with the blue eyes over there, otherwise he'll never let me get to sleep tonight?' he asked her. Paola Miceli, who was spending her holidays at her grandparents' house in Grottaferrata, made the first move. The last time they met each other, Giovanni asked her for her phone number, and got it. What followed were telephone conversations that lasted hours – and thirty-six-hour-long trips to Rome from Milan. He would travel to Rome on a Sunday afternoon in his Aurelia car and return to Milan on Monday evening. Four years later, on 3 June 1964, they got married in the San Nilo Convent in Grottaferrata. 'Outmanoeuvred by a gorgeous opponent,' wrote the media, but Trapattoni was happy to lose this 'duel'. When they met, he had been playing in the national team, but by the time they got married he was already an 'old boy'. They discovered a small paradise on the Tyrrhenian coast called Talamone during their honeymoon and spent some time there.

Back in 1960, during the Olympic year, Trapattoni was selected for the national team and won his first full international cap. On 10 December, Italy were defeated in Naples 1–2 by an Austrian team that included Gerhard Hanappi. While this was the first time that Giovanni Trapattoni played in the 'Azzurri' jersey, it was the last time for the captain, Giampiero Boniperti. Trapattoni's performance was praised by the media: for years, no one had seen such enthusiasm on the field, said the *Gazetta*; it was just too bad about the dozens of missed scoring opportunities. The Lombardian only had a few moments of glamour and glory, and actually experienced more disappointments. In 1962, he was selected to play in the World Cup in Chile, together with six other Milan players. He travelled with them to South America but, due to an ankle injury, wasn't fully fit. He had incurred the injury at the last championship game in Ferrara and he spent the time at the team camp recuperating rather than preparing for the tournament. On 13 May, in a friendly against Belgium, he was able to play only until half-time, at which point his foot began to bother him once more.

This was another era – a time when a ruptured ligament or a torn cartilage meant a month-long healing period, if not the end of your career. It was a time in which an ankle injury should have been left to heal naturally. Even so, Trapattoni might have made an appearance in the World Cup finals if the Italian team management had acted more reasonably and thoughtfully in their team selection for their second match, against Chile, on 2 June 1962, the Italian national holiday. Instead of selecting a team of proven players, a relatively inexperienced side was sent out on to the field, without the time-tested goalie Lorenzo Buffon, without the monumental defender Cesare Maldini, and even without Omar Sivori and Gianni Rivera. The South Americans went after the Italian team and, with some apparently lenient refereeing from the Englishman Ken Aston, won 2–0, with the two goals coming late on in the match. In one fell swoop, in a game which was given the nickname 'the Battle of Santiago', Chile consigned Italy to third place in the group and eliminated them from the competition. The twenty-three-year-old Trapattoni learnt two things from this time: it doesn't make sense to play people who aren't 100 percent fit, and no opponent should be underestimated. '*Non dire gatto se non l'hai nel sacco,*' Trapattoni said at the time: 'Don't count your chickens before they're hatched.' What the Milan player was left with was the jersey with the number six on it; although it was never actually worn at the World Cup, it was one of the most important souvenirs from his career. Another experience that remained with him was having acted as an acolyte at a Mass in Chile.

Trapattoni and Italy were eliminated in the final sixteen by the Soviet Union on aggregate (0–2 in Moscow, 1–1 in Rome). There were, nonetheless, also positive moments during his team career. Altogether they had twelve wins, two ties and three losses in seventeen games, he struck a winning goal on 9 June 1963 against Austria at the Wiener Prater (final score: 1–0). 'It was a diagonal shot, and as my foot met the ball, I knew that it would be a goal,' he later said. There was also the day of his last appearance in Bologna with the Italian team and their victory against Denmark (3–1). This appearance can be regarded as among the weakest of his career. It was only a year later that he disclosed the secret that it was at that time that his great football crisis had begun, and when he started toying with the idea of giving up the sport due to extreme mental stress.

*

The twelfth of May 1963 was one of the more important days in Trapattoni's playing career: *the* most important day, one could even argue. Brazil, the world champions, were guests at Milan's San Siro Stadium, headed by the star of all stars, Pelé. It was Trapattoni's responsibility to make his life difficult. Yes, Pelé had been injured at a friendly game in France, but he had to play in Milan as well due to the stipulations of his contract. His principal opposing player, with the Italian crowd behind him, was highly motivated. During the first twenty-six minutes, Pelé was unable to make any noteworthy moves. Trapattoni's achievement was praised to the heavens: he was the man who had stopped Pelé, the man who had kept the ball away from Pelé, the man who hadn't allowed Pelé even to touch the ball.

Much of the story is true, but much of it isn't. After twenty-six minutes, the Brazilian was substituted, and Trapattoni then covered the unknown, harmless Quarantinha; Italy won 3–0. After the match, the Lombardians were showered with praise. Gianni Rivera was the brains, Giovanni Trapattoni the strength, some said. Others said that Pelé had been happy to be substituted because he knew that he didn't stand a chance against his opponent. To sum up, on that day Trapattoni was equal to Pelé! Trapattoni, humble as always, distanced himself from the adoration he was starting to receive, and said: 'Trapattoni is Trapattoni, but Pelè is Pelè.' Both knew what had really happened on the twelfth of May.

There were to be another duel between Trapattoni and Pelé that same year: at the Intercontinental Cup final between Milan and Santos. In Milan, what was deemed almost impossible actually came to pass. Trapattoni took a pass from Amarildo Tavares da Silveira on the volley and shot from the edge of the penalty box. The ball bounced once before finding its way past the goalkeeper Gilmar Rinaldi and into the net. It was the most impressive goal that had yet been scored by Trapattoni, concluded the experts. Pelé scored twice, once with a penalty kick, but AC still won the first game 4–2 – on a waterlogged pitch. The return game, in South America, was shaping up to be just a formality, but it turned out differently. The referee, Juan Brozzi, let the Santos players play a very physical game, and AC lost the match 2–4. During the replay, Brozzi made more use of the whistle, and awarded a penalty kick to Santos. The penalty was converted by Dalmo Gaspar, and Milan lost the game 0–1.

In order to secure a spot in the World Club Finals (a competition that Trapattoni would win in 1969 against Estudiantes de Buenos Aires, 3–0 and 1–2), the team first had to win the European Cup. AC Milan achieved this on 22 May 1963 in Wembley Stadium, against Benfica and their star Eusébio. Once again, a defender was at the heart of their victory. At the beginning, the Peruvian Victor Morales Benitez was Eusébio's marker, and was overwhelmed with this responsibility. After eighteen minutes, the Portuguese were 1–0 up. Cesare Maldini was reorganising the marking on the field. 'You go cover Eusébio,' he ordered Trapattoni, and the coach, Nereo Rocco, said nothing against it from the bench. Following this tactical measure, Eusébio's spirit, resourcefulness and imagination faded away. Milan won 2–1.

Almost exactly six years later, on 28 May 1969, the thirty-year-old Trapattoni was, for the second and last time in his career, in the European Cup final. Barcelona took on Ajax of Amsterdam in the Bernabéu Stadium. Johann Cruyff was the new rising star at Ajax, and he would first be marked by another Milan player – Angelo Anquilletti – and once again that player would be overwhelmed. Trapattoni took over the delicate duty of covering the talented twenty-two-year-old, and once again he did not disappoint. Johan Cruyff couldn't affect the outcome of the game any more, and Milan won 4–1, with a hat-trick from Pierino Prati.

Trapattoni had won almost all there was to win at club level: the Italian Cup in 1967 and the Cup Winners' Cup in 1968 in Rotterdam, with a 2–0 victory against a Hamburg SV team that included Uwe Seeler. The Italian championship titles he won in 1962 and 1968 could not have been secured in more contrasting fashion. For the first one, there were misunderstandings between the coach Nereo Rocco and the English ace striker Jimmy Greaves. Greaves scored a brace in an away game against Fiorentina, but Milan lost 2–5. Greaves left Italy having scored nine goals; the Milan players didn't know what would happen next. They had already incurred four losses at this early point in the championship; they were eliminated from the Inter-Cities Fairs Cup (the forerunner to the UEFA Cup) and the Italian Cup. A Brazilian player, Dino Sani, was then hired at a bargain price from Boca Juniors as back-up. He seemed to be just marking time until his retirement, but on 12 November the Milan supporters were witness to what they regarded as a miracle:

Sani pulled his socks up and ended up leading his team to a 5–1 win against Juventus and subsequently to the title. The second *scudetto*, six years later, was an improbably easy affair. Ultimately, they had a nine-point lead over SSC Napoli. He won the European Cup in 1963 and 1969, and then the World Club Championship in 1969. He played 284 games in Serie A, and scored just three goals – because he was too selfless, as some would say. (If he had paid more attention to his personal statistics, he might have scored ten goals a season.) Giovanni Lodetti, referred to as Basletta, was, like Trapattoni, a hard, earnest worker on the field. He would become Trapattoni's best friend.

The same fates that took away Trapattoni's mother Romilda, who died at the age of sixty-three on 7 January 1967, would earlier offer him the gift of his first-born daughter, Alessandra, who was born on 31 October 1965. The heavens had not, however, spared the Lombardians from a football crisis. In the 1960s, Inter Milan dominated both nationally and internationally. Trapattoni came up against Luis Suarez, and lost most of the duels. In 1965, Trapattoni thought that he had heart problems and was afraid that he might die. AC Milan practically wrote him off and took his permanent position away from him, placing him on the transfer list. Nereo Rocco's return as coach brought with it Trapattoni's return to the team.

On 23 May 1971, in Rome's Olympic Stadium, Trapattoni played in AC Milan's red-and-black colours for the last time. The game ended 1–1. In the 1971/72 season, he played another ten games in the highest Italian league with FC Varese. On 13 February 1972, he played his last game in Serie A, against AC Torino. His team lost 0–2. In the sixty-third minute, he was substituted for Arrigo Dolso, even though he wasn't injured. Trapattoni, thirty-two, wasn't right for Varese, and vice versa: the provincial club were relegated from Serie A.

And with that, the defender Trapattoni, after twelve years with AC Milan and one season with FC Varese, was himself relegated to the past.

LIFE AS A COACH

AC MILAN
1972–1976

And so it was that Trapattoni moved from the pitch to the coach's bench. It wasn't just somewhere to go after his playing career was finished; it was truly a calling. Trapattoni loved spending his time with the young players, and teaching them the basics of the game – like how one should move on the field, or simply how to stop the ball. He turned down an offer to play in Mantua and instead accepted an offer from Milan to complete his coaching training in Coverciano in Tuscany. Giovanni had learned from his first teacher, Nils Liedholm (a man who was both a father and a psychologist to him), that the coach educates his player. He tried to teach the Scandinavian the Italian language – which was more or less unsuccessful. Then Trapattoni became Nereo Rocco's apprentice. Rocco had brought him back to Milan from Varese in 1972 in order to integrate him into the junior training staff. Rocco, with his Trieste dialect, was known for his straight talking. If there was an important game on the fixture list, he was the first out of the team bus. And before his foot hit the ground, he would turn around and say: 'Whoever's pissing their pants can remain seated. All the rest, follow me!' Giovanni didn't spend long with the junior players. He was quickly deemed worthy of larger responsibilities. However, not all of those at the club agreed with his actions. In 1973, at the end of the season, Nereo Rocco was suspended for three months. He had lost his temper with the referee, Concetto Lo Bello, because he had not given a goal to Milan in a Lazio–Milan match (which Lazio had won 2–1). Rocco's assistant, Cesare Maldini, was sick, and so who had to take the reins for the final match of the season? Giovanni Trapattoni. Now this wasn't a big deal, it should be said: all Italian coaches have to have their first time in the dugout in Serie A at some point. It was just that this was a somewhat tricky situation. At this point in the season, Milan were leading Juventus by one point and had to play in Verona, while the Piedmont team played against AS Roma in Rome. But what must be, must be. AC lost in Romeo and Juliet's city on 20 May 1973, 3–5, and Trapattoni's great ambition, to win the *scudetto*, remained beyond his grasp. Although Juventus were trailing 0–1 after forty-five minutes in Rome, José Altafini evened up the score in the second half. Three minutes before the final whistle, Antonello Cuccureddu scored, giving a final score of 2–1 – and the title win – to Juventus.

In the following season, 1973/74, Cesare Maldini was on the brink of losing his job as coach. He had lost five games in a row in the spring, and finally handed in his notice. Giovanni Trapattoni was once again called in to save the day. He made his first appearance as an official head coach on 14 April 1974 in Milan, against SSC Napoli; the final score was a poor 0–0. It was a mediocre season for AC Milan in the European Cup too; that said, the holders, Borussia Mönchengladbach, were also eliminated, along with Berti Vogts. And on 8 May 1974, AC Milan lost their final game, against Magdeburg in Rotterdam, 0–2 – the first time a team from East Germany had had a big win in the competition. Trapattoni was replaced; the following year, AC Milan president Albino Buticchi appointed Gustavo Giagnoni coach.

One season later, 1975/76, Giovanni Trapattoni was back. Gianni Rivera, who was the one who was really in control at AC Milan during that time, made his friend the coach and placed Nereo Rocco at his side as advisor. They ended the championship in third place – and then Trapattoni decided on a change of location.

He hadn't actually thought of Turin at the time, but rather of Atalanta Bergamo or Pescara – two teams which played in Serie B. However, a call from Pietro Giuliano, manager of Juventus at the time, changed his plans. A meeting with Giampiero Boniperti at the Hotel La Meridiana, on the main road between Milan and Turin close to Novara, cemented things. Trapattoni talked and talked and talked; in the end, he was successful. The new Juventus coach wasn't Eugenio Bersellini, Nils Liedholm or Bruno Pesaola, but rather a thirty-seven-year-old greenhorn called Giovanni Trapattoni.

JUVENTUS, PART I
1976–1986

Most of the fans, and those who connected with the club, were unimpressed by the appointment of Trapattoni. He had too little experience, they said, he hadn't been successful as a coach, he didn't know the business and, most importantly, he didn't drive a Ferrari. In short, in their eyes he wasn't competent to do the job. After all, Juventus had won three titles in the last five years, and the two titles that they had lost, to Lazio and Torino, were by a very narrow margin. Juventus had decades of tradition behind them. Juventus is the grande dame of Italian football: the best is only barely good enough for the club. Juventus had won numerous championships and cups, but had not won any major international trophy until the mid 1970s. And now someone like Giovanni Trapattoni wants to take Juventus all the way to the very top? Ridiculous!

Trapattoni had been hardened by life, though. He knew that that there are times when the wind is blowing your way, and other times when it is against you. And the club that had recruited him to be their coach wasn't just standing by him but was also giving him a team that he could work well with. Fabio Capello and Pietro Anastasi were sold. As replacements, Roberto Boninsegna and Romeo Benetti were signed up, as well as a player with an angel face, who would become one of Italy's best players: Antonio Cabrini.

Giovanni Trapattoni met his long-time friend Gigi Radice in Turin once again. Twenty years earlier, he had been with him on the AC Milan team. Since, at that time, Trapattoni was underage, with no driver's licence and no money for wheels, Radice used to drive him home in his car. Radice was not employed with Juventus, but rather was the coach of their rivals, Torino, and had just won the championship, with Paolo Pulici, Francesco Graziani, Claudio Sala and others. At the time, he was preparing to defend the title, friendship or no friendship. The race for first place was reserved for the northerners during the 1976/77 season. The duel between Juventus and Torino, 'Juve' against 'Toro', brought the entire city under its spell. Both teams were heading the standings after two days of playing and were allowing themselves few mistakes. Juventus were even able to come back from 2–0 down in the away game against AC Milan and, thanks to goals from by Roberto Bettega (2) and Romeo Benetti, win 3–2. Trapattoni experienced his first defeat at, of all places, the Turin derby, with a 0–2 loss, but it was a small setback. The second tie against AC Torino ended 1–1, with Franco Causio scoring the opening goal, for Juve, and Paolo Pulici equalising less than a minute later, for

Torino. Surprisingly, although Radice had been expected to defend the title, Trapattoni ended up winning the championship, with fifty-one points against Radice's fifty. The tally was an Italian record, in a championship with sixteen teams and only sixty available points. Third place went to Fiorentina, way behind, on thirty-five points.

During this first season under Trapattoni, Juventus also had their first taste of success in Europe. On 18 May, they won the UEFA Cup in Bilbao. Although they lost the tie 1–2 against Athletico, the 1–0 victory in Turin meant that they took the title on the away-goals rule. Juventus's elation was such that the president Giampiero Boniperti – and his fine linen suit – ended up being doused in a shower of champagne. The coach was able to keep his team focused and made sure that the victory party stayed on the sidelines. Four days later, they were to play the last championship round: with a 2–0 win against Sampdoria Genoa, they won the title. On the same night, Trapattoni and Boniperti laid the groundwork for further success.

For Giovanni Trapattoni, this was indeed just the beginning, and not the end. Twelve months later, he won his second championship. Although Juventus were not easily the best team in Serie A, they lost only one match out of thirty. In the European Cup competition, Juventus advanced into the semi-finals, where they won first leg against Piemont 1–0, but they then lost the return leg, in Belgium, 0–1. The game was fiercely competitive, with Juventus, 'che riprende la sua danza con scambi deliziosi' (as TV commentator Bruno Pizzul repeated over and over again): 'performing their exquisite ball-passing dance'.

One of the most elegant performances of the championship would not be rewarded, however. In extra time, Claudio Gentile was sent off the field for handball, which resulted in a penalty, and in the 117th minute Rene Van der Eycken's goal won the game, making the final score 2–0.

Trapattoni had to learn once more that sport is a part of life, and that life – or fate – doesn't stop for the game. In the 1977/78 season, Perugian player Renato Curi passed away during the match between Perugia and Juventus. The dedicated and ambitious coach experienced emotions that went beyond anything that could be imagined. It was in such moments that Trapattoni the coach had to yield to Trapattoni the man.

However, life goes on. It was 1978, the year of the World Cup in Argentina. Nine players were summoned from Juventus. Italy was the only team at this World Cup that was able to defeat the host team (in the preliminary round, 1–0). The Argentinians would end up taking the title. Four years later, six Juventus players would be part of the team that would win 3–1 against Germany in the World Cup final in Madrid.

Trapattoni's philosophy went a long way to making the Italian national team so great during that time. 'Ants win', wrote Ovid in the *Metamorphoses*; this could be Trapattoni's motto. Only those who place one foot in front of the other reach their goal. He went through his training sessions with almost manic exactitude. 'I am like a hammer,' he once said – meaning that he strikes again and again at whatever point needs to be corrected. He is a polisher, that's for sure, but one who also lets a lot of work be done with the ball, one who has a system, and who is successful. Antonio Cabrini supplied the fine-tuning for the technique. Trapattoni made a world-class midfielder out of Marco Tardelli (now Trapattoni's assistant in the Republic of Ireland set-up), and he made a title-winning central defender out of the hulk Sergio Brio. From the beginning, Giovanni Trapattoni was known as the champion of defensive football. That said, Juventus was the team that scored the most goals in the championship, and even the specialist defender Gaetano Scirea made the list of goal-scorers.

Every Thursday, they repeated the same ritual. On a piece of paper, slid underneath Trapattoni's watchband, was written the name of a player who had made some mistake or other during the match the previous Sunday. The technique relating to the mistake would then be drilled especially intensely during training. Trapattoni is exact – painfully so – and he never loses his self-control, even when he flies into a rage. This is part of the Trapattoni system of success.

Italian football was shaken up by a betting scandal in the 1979/80 season (Paolo Rossi, among others, was suspended, initially for three years; the suspension was reduced to two years on appeal), and Juventus went through a difficult time. Halfway through the season, the Turin team were in fifth-last place in the table and concerned that they would be relegated. The coach was being talked about, but Trapattoni believed in himself and the team. He would only step down if the club required him to, he said, and anyway, Juventus were exactly where they belonged. In the second half of the season, they collected twenty-four out of thirty possible points and rose to second place, behind Inter Milan; Juventus were then eliminated in the Italian Cup, however, and in the semi-finals of the Cup Winners' Cup. Trapattoni was left empty-handed.

The following years belonged to him, however. In 1981/82, Trapattoni took the national championship with players like Pietro Fanna, Cesare Prandelli, Domenico Marocchino, Giuseppe Galderisi and Sergio Brio. The competition didn't make things easy for him, though. In 1980, after twenty years of isolation, Italian clubs were again allowed to field foreign players. Liam Brady came to Juventus from Arsenal, but even he wasn't able to do anything about Juventus's mediocre start to the championship. (Brady would later be instrumental in Trapattoni's appointment as Republic of Ireland manager.) The Turin derby could have been the final nail in the coffin for their dreams of the title. Juventus had a 1–0 lead over AC Torino; Marco Tardelli then scored, making it 2–0, but the referee Luigi Agnolin disallowed the goal due to a (passive) offside by Pietro Fanna. Two goals by Francesco Graziani gave Torino the victory, even though the second goal was preceded by a foul by Paolo Pulici on the goalkeeper Dino Zoff. The resulting sparring between the two sides led to player suspensions that were unusually severe for Juventus: Claudio Gentile was banned for four matches, Roberto Bettega for three, and Tardelli and Giuseppe Furino for one. AS Roma had a four-point lead. Was it farewell to the *scudetto*?

Juventus's second-string players kept up the pace in the autumn, however, and in the spring Juventus took the lead in the championship. Then another incident came to light: Roberto Bettega had supposedly tried to bribe the centre-back Pin (of Perugia). The sport's governing body pulled the Juventus player out of the game for one month. 'The truth is, we are disagreeable,' Trapattoni announced. His only real striker was now out of the championship. Despite this, a 0–0 draw with AS Roma and a 1–0 win against SSC Napoli assured Juve of the title again. Trapattoni was entitled to this title even more than the first two, due to the fact it they had been won with dramatically weakened teams, and because he had overcome every kind of obstacle, both on and off the field.

In the following season, Roberto Bettega was seriously injured during a European Cup game against RSC Anderlecht, and was out of the game for months. Trapattoni dealt with the situation wisely: he restructured the team, who had a close run-in against Fiorentina which would only be decided on the last day of the season. During the course of the season, it was announced that the foreign stars Zbigniew Boniek and Michel Platini were to join the club. On 2 May 1982, Paolo Rossi appeared for the first time since his suspension in an official game in the Juventus jersey. He scored one goal in the 5–1 win against Udinese. Juventus and Fiorentina were tied at the top of the table before the final day of the season. While Juventus had to travel to Catanzaro, Fiorentina played in Cagliari, where they drew 0–0. Meanwhile, the reigning champions were awarded a penalty kick, which Brady converted – the same Brady who already knew that his contract wouldn't be extended by Juventus.

Finally, the last of the doubters had begun to believe in Trapattoni. The coach had proven himself to be both a master of his profession and a strong person. He referred to the fact that he was working with human beings, not robots, and his words were backed by his deeds. For example, Trapattoni had no doubt when there was some question as to whether the long-time player Giuseppe Furino, a Juventus symbol from the 1970s whose star was waning, would be given the chance of winning his eighth title. 'Furino plays, he has earned it.' (Furino won his first championship in 1971/72 and his last in 1983/84.) Gianni Agnelli, the top dog at Fiat, and Turin's not-so-secret ruler, liked Trapattoni's character and his leadership on and off the field. He found Trapattoni to be 'intelligent, exact and prepared'. Agnelli, an insomniac, often woke the coach up at around 6.30 AM in order to talk to him about this and that. 'The Germans taught us how to read and write,' he said in a call to him after the final European Cup game against Hamburg SV was lost in 1983. Another time, when Trapattoni requested that Agnelli bring Paolo Rossi to Turin, he received the answer: 'He costs too much. We have thousands of people on the dole. Give me another name.' However, Rossi, as history records, would ultimately become a Juventus player.

After four championships had been won, stars like Platini and Boniek came to Turin, found their place in the team, accepted their subordinate roles, and experienced

Trapattoni in all his perfection. While Platini improved his free kicks after training, a wall of players had to stand there – even in pouring rain. The coach wouldn't accept the players' request that they be replaced by dummies. Trapattoni had some debates with Michel Platini. The Frenchman wanted to have a team that was only geared towards attack. The Italian conceded: 'All right, but first bring me the ball!' And that was when the coach would tell the story over and over again of the soldier who secretly left the enemy camp at night and, the next day, told the General: 'I took thirty prisoners.' 'Really?' 'I swear.' 'I believe you, I believe you. But first, show them to me!' The rigorous workouts, and the long time spent putting his ideas into practice, would be rewarded with success in various competitions. Juventus won the title in 1984 and 1986, secured the Cup Winners' Cup in Basel in May 1984 thanks to a 2–1 win against FC Porto, and set their sights on the greatest prize they had yet to win: the European Cup, which up to this point had been won by only two Italian teams, AC Milan and Inter Milan.

There are two moments that are writ large in the history of football: one due to a surprising outcome, and the other due to the tragedy that occurred as a result of that outcome.

On 23 May 1983, Juventus came up against Hamburg SV in Athens; it was already assumed that they would win the European Cup. There were six world champions in the Italian team, legendary goalkeeper Dino Zoff, World

Cup top-scorer Paolo Rossi, the key player Michel Platini, and the lively striker Zbigniew Boniek among them. The team was supported by forty thousand fans who had travelled there to see them, and who were just waiting to watch Juventus ascend to the throne of European club football. Nothing would come of it, however – a fact that Giovanni Trapattoni was already aware of after a spying trip to northern Germany. (Michel Platini wanted to cheer him up after his return from Germany and told him that even he would be thinking about the Germans – for which he received a compassionate look.) Hamburg's coach, Ernst Happel, had managed Holland in the 1978 World Cup. Holland made it through to the final, where they were beaten by Argentina in extra time. Now, against Juventus, preaching zonal defence, he marshalled his forces well, using Wolfgang Rolff as Platini's marker. The deciding moment came in the ninth minute: Felix Magath shot right over Zoff and into the net. Trapattoni ranted, roared, whistled and yelled instructions at the players for the remaining eighty-one minutes. He replaced Paolo Rossi with Domenico Marocchino, ensuring that they didn't concede any more goals, but the loss stuck in Trapattoni's gut for a long time, and probably still bothers him today.

A few weeks later, he won the Italian Cup, and although it's always nice to win a trophy, it was no substitute for the European Cup. This success, one that would be a demonstration of their will and fighting spirit, still stood before Juventus as a challenge. After a 0–2 loss in Verona, Rossi and Platini were only able to level up the scores in the second leg, towards the end of normal time. And during extra time, in the 119th minute, Platini scored again.

On 29 May 1985, two years and six days after the loss to Hamburg, Juventus went to play Liverpool at Heysel Stadium in Brussels. Trapattoni won the European Cup for the third time, but for the first time as a coach. Platini converted a penalty kick against Liverpool. It seemed that the Swiss referee, André Daina, had only awarded the penalty in order to avoid extra time for himself and the teams, as the foul had actually occurred outside the penalty box; no one from the English team had protested.

But what happened on the pitch during that game was really immaterial. It was an evening of disgrace and misery for European football. What is a win worth, or a loss, when thirty-nine people are dead on the field and hundreds are injured? Liverpool fans had spilled into the Italian fans' section, and panic broke out. In the general agitation, people were trampled to death. Afterwards, both teams still had to make their appearance on the field. They played '*con il cuore a pezzi*', 'with their hearts in pieces' – and only to avoid something worse happening. The Juve captain, Platini, was criticised for the fact that he raised the cup in the air in an expression of victory. He was later quoted as saying: 'When the tightrope walker falls in the circus, it's time for the clowns to come in.' What happened on that evening was not a final of the most popular sport in the world, but rather a surreal theatre that included elements of both war and sport.

Heysel in spring, an idyllic scene. People are strolling through the parks, under the Atomium, going to the cinema, to the pools. There is an easy-going mood around the King Baudouin stadium, the stadium that people still know by its former name, Heysel, after the neighbourhood. In Brussels, Heysel is a synonym for a nice afternoon. In other European countries, it is synonymous with tragedy.

On the twentieth anniversary of the event, a monument will finally be erected to commemorate the thirty-nine people who died on 29 May 1985, a day that changed football forever. It will be a sixty-square-metre sundial, which will stand in memory of those who were killed. The memory of that Tuesday is already gaining focus again, eight weeks before the sad anniversary, because for the first time since that match Liverpool and Juventus are once again competing against each other. The game is supposed to be an act of reconciliation.

Contemporary witnesses were interviewed by various media groups, and their perceptions illustrate how much football and safety regulations have changed since Heysel, the day when football's Middle Ages ended. Thirty-nine spectators, thirty-two of whom were Italians, died, and more than four hundred were injured when a horde of Liverpool supporters invaded Section Z. People fled in panic, and since they were unable to find a way out, they broke down a wall. Most of the victims were smothered to death there.

Though there had already been football catastrophes, this one was the first to be shown live on television in seventy-seven countries. Only German television stopped transmission of the game. And that was not all that happened which would seem unimaginable today. There were no weapons controls, ticket sales were lax (which meant that many Italians went into the 'neutral' Section Z), and eight police officers and a thin wire fence were the only buffer between sections. There was no video surveillance. It was a truly dilapidated stadium. And this carelessness was after the hate-filled final in Rome, where English fans, without police protection, were subjected to violence from Italian fans.

After the horrific scene had long been played for the whole world to see, the starting whistle for the Heysel final was blown – after an eighty-five-minute delay. 'We were forced to do it,' said Paolo Rossi bitterly. 'I don't have the feeling that I won this cup. Juventus should give it back, out of respect for the dead.' Like most of the players, above all Juventus, who after their 1–0 win went on a lap of honour, he asserted that the players had not realised the extent of the situation in the locker room. 'We only realized it after the game.'

His teammate Zbigniew Boniek, speaking through Reuters, contradicted what Rossi had said about the incident: 'We knew 99.9 percent of what was happening, from the deaths and the dynamic situation, to the explosive atmosphere in the stadium. I repeat: We knew it all.' Liverpool's captain Phil Neal also confirmed this. 'The players knew that there had been deaths. We should never have played. UEFA were insistent that the violence could continue if we didn't play.'

The head of the Red Cross at the time, Jacques Van Camp, defended that decision: 'Otherwise there wouldn't have only been thirty-nine deaths, but rather hundreds of deaths and thousands of people injured.' English clubs were subsequently banned from the European Cup for five years – something from which they still haven't recovered. In the eight years before Heysel, they had won the cup four times; since then, only once. Fourteen hooligans were imprisoned. It was only in 1992 that a Brussels court ruled that UEFA functionaries, as well as the police, were also partly responsible for the tragedy.

The catastrophes in both Heysel and Hillsborough (in 1989, ninety-five fans died in Sheffield) redefined stadium security, and led to a new boom in the number of spectators. But not everywhere. While in England football was once again discovered as a pleasure that could be enjoyed without fear, the experience in Heysel still caused Italy to remain subdued.

Otello Lorentini had to watch his thirty-year-old son Roberto die at Heysel while trying to save a young girl's life. 'The English are the only ones who were able to learn something from it. Thatcher was brave enough to do what no Italian government would do against violence in football,' said the founder of the group established for the families of the victims. That is why, in England and elsewhere, there are now 'safer stadiums, while in Italy we are still afraid to take our children to the game'.

Michel Platini won't go to the stadium any more – whether they call it Heysel or King Baudouin. He was 'not in the physical or mental state for it'. If he wanted to become the UEFA president, however, he would have to. The candidate would go down the Anfield Road on Tuesday and eight days later be in the Stadio Delle Alpi with a political message: 'It is a deep wound, one that cannot be healed. However, it is time to turn the page.' That is why we should 'make the game a celebration, like it should have been that day'. His appeal to the fans was: 'Is there any better opportunity to bring peace back to football?'

5 APRIL 2005, CHRISTIAN EICHLER

Trapattoni had matured. The player, the actor on the field, was henceforth the coach, the director on the sidelines. One could even call him a commander, in keeping with the war-like theme of the aforementioned events. The events ate away at him, and he tried to work through it, because he knew that life would go on. On 8

December 1985, he celebrated another success with Juventus at the World Club final in Tokyo against the Argentinian Boca Juniors. It was a match that not only drove the Japanese spectators wild but also made the Brazilian, Leovegildo Lins da Gama Junior, who was at the time under contract with AC Torino, arrive at an enthusiastic conclusion: he had never seen such a fantastic match in his life. Juventus equalised twice, got through extra time unscathed, and secured the victory with the last spot-kick of the penalty shoot-out. The mosaic was complete. In a single decade, Trapattoni had won everything with Juventus that there was to win: six Italian Championships, two Italian Cups (1979 and 1983), all three European cup competitions, the World Club Championship and the UEFA Cup (1984, 2–0 against Liverpool). He had accumulated 423 points in 300 championship matches; that is also a record.

Trapattoni therefore decided that ten years were enough, and that he needed a new challenge. He decided to go back to where he had come from: Milan. Another motivating factor was his wife's desire to move back there. He didn't decide to weigh anchor on the red-and-black shores of AC Milan, though, but rather on the black-and-blue of Inter. Juventus's functionaries were disbelieving, and unwilling to accept the news. The coach informed Giovanni Agnelli at the last possible moment; he didn't want to give anyone the opportunity to convince him to stay. Agnelli admitted defeat. However, he did still ask Mrs Trapattoni: 'Why are you taking him away from us?' And to the coach, he said: 'Just don't forget, I will always see Juventus's coach in you.'

INTER MILAN
1986–1991

At the beginning of the twenty-first century, it has become common practice in the professional – and sometimes mercenary – football business to change teams from year to year and also to move to places far away from where one had originated. Whereas at the end of the last century, it wasn't just about titles and cups, but rather about *appartenenza* – belonging to a club. A person would commit himself heart and soul to the club for his entire life. He wouldn't want to have anything to do with any other club, and he certainly wouldn't want to employ their players or their coach.

Giovanni Trapattoni, on the contrary, received a wave of sympathy upon his arrival at Inter Milan, and for good reason. The successful Juventus coach was meant to take Inter Milan back up to the top at long last. The last time they had won the championship was in 1980, and the last international trophy, the European Cup, had been won in 1965. The Inter fans were hungry: hungry for success, and hungry to be able once again to hold conversations in cafés about their victories. '*Noi dell'Inter, voi del Milan.*' ('We from Inter, you from Milan.')

The messiah only needed ninety minutes at the beginning of the 1986/87 championship season to realise that Inter Milan was truly a different club, a different team. A star-studded team that included Karl-Heinz Rummenige, Alessandro Altobelli and Daniel Passarella lost 0–1 in Florence on 24 September 1986 to the provincial team Empoli, thanks to a goal by Marco Osio. A month later, the Milan derby ended 0–0, and from then on Inter couldn't catch SSC Napoli. (Diego Maradona was the talisman for Napoli that day.) All was lost after the 1–2 defeat to AC Milan in the return fixture. Inter finished in the bottom third of the table, although this situation was blamed more on the coach than on the players.

The second season with Inter Milan didn't bring Trapattoni the *scudetto* either. It began with a 0–2 loss at the San Siro Stadium against Pescara, which started a rebellion among the older stars. In the Pescara game, Massimo Ciocci was brought on to replace Altobelli after seventy-three minutes. Inflamed with rage, Altobelli hurled his captain's armband in the coach's face. Trapattoni lost both derbys and had to watch the Milan coach, Arrigo Sacchi (whose views on football he didn't share), experience a sensational comeback.

Trapattoni was greatly affected by Sacchi's title win because Sacchi was a media darling who used completely different tactics: he was known as the prophet of the zone-defence system. So this victory rankled with him, in the same way as some losses for his own team rankled with him. However, Trapattoni was amenable to change,

Trapattoni silencing his critics

Trapattoni and Angelo Di Livio at the 2002 World Cup

Ezequiel Carboni of Red Bull Salzburg challanging Brad Friedel of Blackburn Rovers in the 2006 UEFA Cup

Celebrating winning the Austrian League in 2007

Trapattoni keeps his team on their toes.

Gianluigi Buffon, Italian goalkeeper in the 2002 and 2006 World Cups

© Getty Images

The Juventus team celebrating winning the 1993 UEFA Cup by raising Trapattoni on their shoulders. They won 6–1 on aggregate.

© Getty Images

'Not once but twice': A linesman takes the brunt of Trapattoni's anger.

Mehmet Scholl (top) and Thomas Strunz, two players singled out by Trapattoni in a famous press-conference outburst in March 1998. Trapattoni claimed they were not pulling their weight in the Bayern Munich team.

Trapattoni 'developed his leopard walk; he would stalk along the sidelines and be continously expelled by the animal trainer – in other words, the linesman'.

Alessandro del Piero, the highest-earning Italian player, who was given his first Serie A game in 1993 for Juventus by Trapattoni. Del Piero would later feel under-appreciated in comparison to Totti when Trapattoni was managing the national team in the 2002 World Cup.

Trapattoni gets his point across.

Trapattoni training with Stuttgart in Dubai

Trapattoni and Othmar Hitzfeld, manager of Bayern Munich

Holding the Austrian league trophy

Giovane Elber and Trapattoni celebrate Bayern Munich winning the German Cup in 1998

Lothar Matthäus and Trapattoni have words with linesman Fritz Stuchlik.

Banners honouring Trapattoni and Matthäus at Red Bull Salzburg's stadium

Filippo Inzaghi, the all-time leading goal-scorer in the UEFA Champions League. He was also the top goal-scorer for Italy at the 2002 World Cup.

and together with Inter president Ernesto Pellegrini, he changed the image, name and equipment of the club, which had been founded in 1908. Daniel Passarella, Enzo Scifo and Alessandro Altobelli were transferred in the summer of 1988, and Lothar Matthäus, Andreas Brehme, Nicola Berti, Alessandro Bianchi and Ramon Diaz were signed up. The Algerian Rabah Madjer, or 'Allah's heel' (because of a back-heel he had made for FC Porto in the European Cup final in 1987 against Bayern), was on the coach's wish-list as well; however, due to physical problems, they had to change their plans.

Despite these additions to the squad, Trapattoni's third year at Inter also brought defeat. On 28 September, Fiorentina, thanks to a 4–3 win, dumped Inter out of the Italian Cup. On 7 December, the Milan players lost 1–3 in the second leg of a UEFA Cup tie against Bayern Munich, following a seven-minute spell in which Bayern scored three times. The first leg, which they had won at the Olympic Stadium, was rendered worthless due to the away-goals rule.

It was only in the league that Inter were in a class of their own: Walter Zenga in goal, Giuseppe Bergomi and Riccardo Ferri in defence, Andrea Mandorlini, Andreas Brehme on the left flank, Alessandro Bianchi on the right, Nicola Berti and Lothar Matthäus as attacking midfielders, Gianfranco Matteoli as a steadying force, and Ramon Diaz and Aldo Serena as strikers. These were all names that drove opponents to despair in the 1988/89 season. It was important to Trapattoni to adhere to his concept of being tactical and defence-minded; he continually had to hold back his players' forward drive. 'Attack, mister, attack!' yelled Matthäus at the bench. And in answer, he would get: 'Stay where you are, it's better that way.' The relationship between the playmaker on the field and the one on the bench wasn't always free of friction, but Trapattoni knew how to deal with players – and people. 'He understands the psychological make-up of each individual as well as of the team as a whole,' said Aldo Serena, the top scorer of that year, 'and even if he occasionally comes down as hard as iron, he still figures out the right approach for each person.'

He talked to Walter Zenga for hours when the latter had the opportunity to accept a lucrative offer from Naples, and in the end the goalkeeper stayed in Milan. Giovanni Trapattoni lived in a villa in Cusano Milanino, his birthplace. He went to church every Saturday evening and then visited the players in their rooms, with God at his side. He spoke to each of them in order to let them know what the schedule was and to talk to them about their performance. During his five years with Inter Milan, he developed his 'leopard walk'; he would stalk along the sidelines and be continuously expelled by the 'animal trainer' – in other words, the linesman.

Nineteen eighty-nine proved to be Inter's year. It was a season in which the Milan players were on the top of the table from beginning to end. They won the derby against AC Milan and Arrigo Sacchi 1–0 and went sixteen rounds in Serie A without being knocked down. Inter's seventeenth league match, an away game with Fiorentina, and their star Roberto Baggio, was lost 3–4. The coach went into a rage and yelled in the locker room, like Nereo Rocco had once done. 'Any of you who are in this room right now and don't believe that we can win the title, should get lost, and now!' No one moved. No one dared to breathe. Everyone believed. The second championship defeat came in the latter half of the season, 0–2 against AC Torino, who were embroiled in a struggle against relegation at the time. However, at this point Inter Milan were already almost assured of the championship. The numbers were impressive. Twenty-six wins in thirty-four matches, fifty-eight points, sixty-seven goals, nineteen against, Aldo Serena the top-scorer with twenty-two goals. Their lead over the second-placed SSC Napoli was eleven points. Their lead over the third-placed team, Milan, was twelve points. (The AC Milan fans also had reason to celebrate; twenty years after the last title win in which Giovanni Trapattoni had also taken part, their team won the Coppa Italia.)

In the following two seasons, Inter Milan came third in the championship, but they were at least able to win the UEFA Cup in 1991, with a 2–0 win and a 0–1 loss away to AS Roma. On 22 May of that year, Giovanni Trapattoni informed them that he would be leaving. He and the president, Ernesto Pellegrini, had come to an understanding, and they were terminating his contract. Milan, said Trapattoni, was like a washing machine. 'It tosses you around and spits you out as a rag.' That may have been. What is clear, however, is that Trapattoni moved back to Turin and soon received a call from Gianni Agnelli, '*l'avvocato*'.

It may be that, while searching for a challenge, Trapattoni realised that he wouldn't be able to break down AC Milan's dominance over Inter Milan. Juventus had laid an offer on the table, and the remuneration was right: 1.3 billion instead of 950 million lire (or €650,000 instead of €475,000 in today's money). Although the relationship between Inter Milan and Trapattoni had cooled, both sides were still tied together until the spring of 1992 by the contract. The result was a unique situation that later became commonplace. Inter wanted to get rid of Trapattoni anyway, and already had a replacement waiting on the sidelines: Corrado Orrico. However, they didn't want to release the successful coach from his duties without receiving some kind of compensation; Pellegrini wanted players from Juventus. The new coach–player market had been opened. Trapattoni burst into a rage; it was an absurd request, and he felt insulted. The result: he would never stay with Inter. Pellegrini followed this with: 'Our coach next year? Why, Trapattoni, of course.' And then, the response: 'That possibility is ruled out. It's not about the money for me, for all I care; I just won't coach for one year.'

Around this time, Trapattoni went into business – with a friend, Pasquale Piccolo, and some other associates. He opened an auto-repair and spare-parts shop. The friendship between the two dated back to the Lombardian's years as a player. It deepened during the time that both men had worked in Turin, when they met each other almost every day for breakfast in the café. Piccolo had seen the coach as he shouted Zbigniew Boniek off the field because he had hurled a ball over the barrier out of anger and frustration, and then yelled after the Polish player: 'And if you don't like it, you can complain to the lawyer, to Agnelli.' Now he experienced an agreeable, friendly person, who liked to talk about many different things. But there was one subject he would not broach: his work. For Trapattoni knew that every Italian thought that he knew everything about football. However, when it comes to expressing an opinion, no one can do it as resolutely as Trapattoni. Once, when the team manager was trying to convince an injured player to play again by giving him a shot and a schnitzel, the coach aggressively refused, to the point where the others had to be quiet and let him have his way. His role at the auto-repair shop was very different. In the advertisement for it, they show Trapattoni looking over his mechanic's shoulder, with a slogan hanging on the wall: '*Centro più scudettato d'Italia*' – 'The autoshop with the most Italian championships'.

JUVENTUS, PART II
1991–1994

Gianni Agnelli, Turin's overlord, had to intervene in the dealings between Juventus and Inter in order to untie the Gordian knot. Ernesto Pellegrini prevailed in the end and got one player from Juventus, Dino Baggio. Trapattoni went back to Turin, where most people loved and honoured him, and was reunited with his old comrade-in-arms, Agnelli, with whom he could make plans for future triumphs. In Turin, though, there were also fans who were more interested in reproaching him for the four lost championships than in rejoicing over the six titles they had won with him. And still others claimed that he was old news, and wondered whether he was still a good coach.

Regardless, Giovanni Trapattoni was back where he belonged. He had even sat on the home-team bench when he was with Inter Milan and they had been playing a match at the Turin *Comunale*.

The duel with AC proved to be difficult. He at least

won 2–1 against Inter on 8 December 1991. However, when he lost 0–2 against his friend and coaching colleague, Emiliano Mondonico, in Florence on 26 January 1992, the dream of the title was lost. And there was more disappointment to come. Juventus, with Jürgen Kohler, Júlio Cesár da Silva, Pierluigi Casiraghi and Roberto Baggio, eliminated Inter in the quarter-finals and Milan in the semi-finals of the Italian Cup. They then won the first leg of the final, against Parma, 1–0, but the second leg went to Parma, with a 2–0 win. Trapattoni came away empty-handed.

AC Milan made a quick start the following season, with seven wins. They beat Juventus 1–0, thanks to a goal by Marco Simone, and by the middle of the championship they had a twelve-point lead over their greatest rival. Although it was too late, Trapattoni enjoyed a 3–1 win against AC Milan in the return leg, through a great team effort, and won a place in the UEFA Cup. Juventus defeated Benfica in the quarter-finals, Paris St Germain (with George Weah) in the semi-finals and Borussia Dortmund, who were coached by Ottmar Hitzfeld, in the finals. The first leg in Germany was a clear win, 3–1; although Borussia took the lead, with a goal from Michael Rummenigge Junior, first Dino Baggio and then Roberto Baggio (with two goals) scored, setting up the win. The second leg in Turin was even more emphatic: a 3–0 win for Juventus.

This would, however, be the only title that Trapattoni won during his second spell with Juventus. In 1993/94 the goal difference went to Juve (plus thirty-three, as opposed to plus twenty-one), but the points went to

Milan (fifty, as opposed to forty-seven). Trapattoni sur-rendered the battle against AC, thought about the squad, and concluded that one couldn't make good wine with-out good grapes. He also recognised that the public's cri-teria for evaluating a coach had changed. Those who had a reputation for being conservative said that it didn't mat-ter what technical or tactical skills you provided, but rather what kind of show you could offer. AC Milan characterised Trapattoni as 'the product of successful propaganda' and could refer to how he had given many first chances to the big names in Italian football: Angelo Di Livio, whom he preferred to the well-established Paolo Di Canio, or Alessandro del Piero, who was given his first Serie A game by Trapattoni, on 12 September 1993 – as a replacement for Fabrizio Ravanelli after sev-enty-three minutes.

However, other job prospects were calling: the Germans, for example. Trapattoni was contacted by Bayern Munich.

BAYERN MUNICH, PART I
1994–1995

The time was ripe for a new challenge, for a new country. Giovanni Trapattoni had worked as a coach in Italy for seventeen years and had won sixteen titles. He had in fact won everything that a club coach could win. 'There was nothing there to excite me any more.'

The call from FC Bayern came just at the right time. The club was the best that the German national league had to offer. And Trapattoni, who had long been called '*il tedesco*' – 'the German' – in Italy, had always had a weakness for German football and German players, 'because of their mentality, character and quality'. The record-holding champions had had their ups and downs in the last few years. However, despite having had four coaches in three years, they had still won the German championship, with Franz Beckenbauer as interim coach, after a long time without collecting any silverware.

It was a tall order for Trapattoni to follow Beckenbauer. The latter had a reputation for being successful at everything he set his mind to. Without even a coaching licence, he had led the national team to the World Cup title as team manager and had got FC Bayern back on top of the national scene. He was the ideal coach for many fans, but he didn't feel like working on the field any more. It was no problem for Trapattoni to succeed the popular Beckenbauer. 'I'm happy to carry the burden.' And who else had the charisma, the competence and the authority to walk in the footsteps of 'the Kaiser'?

Trapattoni was 'presented' in Munich shortly after the end of the 1993/94 season. Bayern president Fritz Scherer praised him as a 'stroke of luck' for the newly crowned champions. 'There couldn't be any better person after Beckenbauer.' Trapattoni signed a year-long contract, with a one-sided option for the club. He only wanted to be kept on in the position for as long as the Bayern club was convinced of the quality of his work and his grasp of football. He declined a longer contract – which is rather unusual given that this was a time when severance packages were fought for.

Trapattoni met old acquaintances in Bayern. He had trained Karl-Heinz Rummenigge, now the vice-president in Bayern, and Lothar Matthäus, the sweeper, when they were with Inter Milan. Although he had felt that Rummenigge was past his best and had fought some battles with Matthäus, they both had very high opinions of him. The feelings were also mutual. Trapattoni promoted Matthäus to be his key player on the field and praised him highly. He was a winner, he said, and stated that 'You can already call him my favourite player'.

Six weeks later, Trapattoni had his first working day

with FC Bayern. He had the players train intensively for two hours. The following weeks would be hard for the Munich team. The new coach didn't place value only on power and conditioning, but above all on technique and tactics. 'In my country, they train with more adaptability,' he would say. 'The players are more flexible, and that gives them greater technical strength when it comes to controlling the ball.' He was therefore trying to communicate a little bit of the Italian game's culture to the Germans – just as he had earlier tried to bring some German discipline to his Italian team.

Practice under Trapattoni usually lasted longer than was normal for German teams: two hours, sometimes even two and a half. The Bayern professionals were not used to that. They stretched, hopped and juggled both with and without the ball, and tackling was practised much less than before. In addition, the new coach improved on tactical performance, interrupted the exercises over and over again in order to improve the players, and made them repeat the exercises until he was happy with the results, until everything was as it should be. It was mostly about nuances for the perfectionist Trapattoni, who called these hours 'practical tactical education'. He made the players practise pressing often, with four defenders against five attackers. One side had to learn to pass the ball at the right moment, and the other side had to learn how to keep a good shape. They had almost no normal practice games.

Trapattoni was also known in his country as an avid tactical specialist. He had witnessed the development of the game in Italy over the last half-century, and this resulted in him having a clear idea of how the teams had to act, either with or without the ball. Trapattoni would later write a book with a football professor entitled *The Conception and Development of Football Tactics*. In it, he describes 'his' football, how various components have to be combined to secure a win. Precision, fast implementation, complete technical mastery, intelligence, creative autonomy, setting, technical skills and tactical principles are crucial. Later, when he became the coach of the '*squadra azzurra*', it would be suggested that he was particularly defence-oriented. He continuously has had to fight this preconception. In his book, he describes different perceptions of what attack-oriented football is. Brazil is considered to be an attacking team because the players make contact with the ball so often, without losing it, and this necessarily leads to a great deal of possession of the ball. However, a goal-kick by the goalkeeper is also a contribution to an attacking move. What is crucial for him is that the players play in the opponents' half of the pitch, far away from their own goal.

Above all, the young Bayern players were enthusiastic about Trapattoni's 'school'. 'After every training session, you have the impression that you have improved again,' said Christian Nerlinger. Jorginho, the freshly chosen Brazilian world champion, was also delighted. 'Finally, we have a coach who is improving our tactical skills.' Trapattoni would sometimes select one player at the end of the practice and work with him for thirty or forty minutes longer. Matthäus remembered his time at Inter, when he often had the pleasure of these special sessions. 'I was already a national player and a German champion.

But two or three times a week, Trapattoni would take me aside and train my left foot. It paid off.'

All the same, the beginning of Trapattoni's career in Munich was a bit bumpy. Trapattoni won his first German title, the not very highly regarded Fuji Cup. However, three days later, Bayern lost the Super Cup final to Werder Bremen. 'We are never going to play like that again,' promised Trapattoni. If this loss was hard to cope with, the next one was even harder. Before the start of the national competition, the first round of the DFB Cup was held. Lots were drawn, and it was decided that Bayern would play against a club from a village in Franconia with just 350 inhabitants: the third-league team TSV Vestenbergsgreuth. Winning should have been a simple task, but the champions were 0–1 down to the amateurs at half-time, and they failed to make good the deficit in the second half. Their chances of winning the Cup were lost. This wasn't the first embarrassment in the cup competition for Bayern; they had also lost four years earlier against another amateur club.

Trapattoni could see that there was a great deal of work to be done. 'The team gave their all, but they have to learn to read the game better when the opponents are closing in on them.' It dawned on him for the first time that all that glitters is not gold, and that this was perhaps the case with FC Bayern. 'If I stay longer, some things have to change,' he asserted; in particular, he found fault with 'organisational problems'. What exactly he meant by that, he wouldn't say.

The team did indeed win at the beginning of the national-league season, but the 'Maestro' was not placat-

ed by the performance against Bochum. The success did-
n't come from their organisation – at least not from the
type of organisation that Trapattoni had already spent
weeks teaching them. A lot happened by chance, and that
wasn't enough for him. Trapattoni gesticulated wildly,
constantly jumped up from his spot on the bench, and
took much more of his temper out on the sidelines than
on the team on the field. Once, he even head-butted the
oversized fruit-drink advertisement that was next to the
bench. And of course he whistled often. However, apart
from Matthäus, no one seemed to know what he wanted
to say. The Bayern captain explained what the meaning of
his whistling was afterwards. He said that, when
Trapattoni uses his little fingers as an aid, it means that
'we are playing too closely to one side, and that we have
to shift the action of the game'.

Trapattoni considered Bayern's playing style to be too
individualistic; he wanted to see a greater degree of teamwork and was hoping that, with his encouragement, the
players would develop a better understanding of the
game. He knew that this couldn't happen overnight,
though. An Italian saying, and one that the coach was
fond of, goes: 'It takes nine months for a person to be
born.' He of course didn't have that much time with
Bayern, and a setback in Freiburg, a 1–5 thrashing,
sparked off the first criticisms. The criticism did not
come from the higher-ups at FC Bayern, however. Three
highly competent former professional players, Uli
Hoeneß as manager, as well as the chairmen, Karl-Heinz
Rummenigge and Franz Beckenbauer, were all in agreement, and their words carried some weight among the

public. The trio was asserting that the players were responsible for the failure, not the coach. President Fritz Scherer's intervention, however, caused a good deal of confusion. He mentioned that Beckenbauer could speak with some of the younger players and use his influence as Germany's guiding light. The Bayern president quickly had to back-pedal, and stressed that Beckenbauer would not by any means encroach into Trapattoni's domain.

In his first couple of weeks in the job, the Italian had already got his first insight into the FC Bayern world – a world which was quite unique due to the team's hugely impressive record in the league. Everything, even the smallest side notes, took on colossal importance when it had something to do with the German champions. Sometimes even the most insignificant events that occurred at the club would be given whole pages in the newspaper. Trapattoni had to take some time to get used to the German media, given that they differed so much from Italy.

Trapattoni set a minimal goal for the team in that year's Champions League: to reach the quarter-finals. Those upstairs weren't even dreaming of getting closer to the top-ranked clubs, like FC Barcelona or AC Milan, after such a long period away from this level of competition. Bayern's vice-president didn't give them much reason to hope that the team could make it through the group stage. 'We're starting from point zero once again,' reported Rummenigge after the 0–2 loss to Paris Saint Germain. Trapattoni thought that disharmony in the team's structure was the cause of the unsuccessful trip to France, which had already destroyed their hopes of being allowed back into the circle of great European champions. The old hands were at the back, and the inexperienced greenhorns in the front, which wasn't right. He therefore raised the option once again of switching Lothar Matthäus back into the centre of the action and away from the sweeper position. As the captain, he could then pull the strings and direct the young talent. Trapattoni insisted on this tactical direction. Matthäus, who was now thirty-three years old, let it be known that he would prefer to play at the back so that he could better ration his strength. Especially since he had just come back after an exhausting World Cup tournament and was not yet quite match-fit.

Trapattoni's job at FC Bayern was more difficult than he thought it would be. He had to build up as many young players as possible, and yet at the same time not diminish the assets they already had – something which was of course practically impossible. The club was therefore not satisfied with the level of success they had achieved. Furthermore, sometimes it seemed as though it was simply a problem of comprehension, when the players were once again failing to do what the coach was asking of them. Trapattoni of course had the help of a translator at his side, but he often waved his help away on the field. He had a private teacher and took German lessons regularly; he was soon able to speak to the team in his Italian-English-German pidgin. Those who wanted to, knew what the 'Maestro' wanted with his 'Trapattonian', but at some point the experienced players couldn't get anything out of the tactical training any more. They began to grumble, at first quietly and inter-

nally, and later they began to express out loud and publicly what was going wrong for them. They were watching their own very German abilities – namely their tackling strength – slowly deteriorating in the face of
Trapattoni's unusual training methods. There were soon
the first indications that Trapattoni would indeed not be
extending his contract at the end of the season – particularly because the club management was no longer sure if
they had found the right man for the team. Beckenbauer,
who had in the meantime been promoted to president of
the club, had let it be known while he was performing his
side job as a television commentator that he didn't want
to watch these boring Bayern football games any more.
'We're playing scaredy-cat football.' He didn't want to
attack Trapattoni by saying such things, but rather considered it to be the fault of the players, who were, he
thought, too 'boring, calculating and cautious'. However,
this could of course also have been seen as a gentle criticism of the coach. Regardless of the fact that Bayern
reached the Champions League quarter-finals,
Beckenbauer announced that he wanted to change FC
Bayern's face for the new season – by which he meant the
team, not Trapattoni, at least initially.

Trapattoni was starting to feel like moving on. His
wife was already ready to go back to Italy – and today
rather than tomorrow. However, it was not because she
didn't feel comfortable in Munich. The Trapattonis had
an apartment in the centre of the city with a view of the
Frauenkirche, just a stone's throw from the opera house.
They were both music lovers, but Trapattoni could find
time neither for his hobby nor for building a new circle

of friends. What with learning the language as well, he was busy with FC Bayern practically around the clock. Their son Alberto was having trouble meeting school requirements, since the students in Germany were more advanced in some subjects than they were in Italy. Regardless of what happened at the club, Paola would move back to Italy in the summer with their son so that he could get a good grade in his final exams.

And then, on top of everything else, there was the language problem. 'It suddenly occurred to me that at my age I would never learn German quickly enough to be able to hold a press conference alone, that I couldn't become 100 percent effective.' During the winter break, he spoke often in Italy about leaving Germany. This news spread quickly, and of course was made public on the other side of the Alps. Bayern were pushing for a decision, which Trapattoni finally made. He may have made the decision a little too fast, he later admitted, since he had also let himself be influenced by the chaotic situation in December. 'If the club had dealt with this situation more calmly, perhaps I would have been willing to stay,' he later said.

During the winter break, he publicly remained silent, and vehemently ignored the rumours, even refusing to give press conferences. Bayern had known about his decision for a while, however, and were already trying to find a successor – without making much of an effort to hide the fact. Otto Rehhagel, a coach who had celebrated much success with Werder Bremen in the past years, was scheduled to come to Munich in the summer. In as far as his basic understanding of tactical strategy was concerned, he wasn't in fact much different from his Italian colleague.

When, at the start of the second half of the season, Trapattoni disclosed what everyone had been anticipating, Bayern took the opportunity to announce the new man. The rumour was that there might be a change in the dugout even before the end of the season. Given that he was on his way out anyway, Trapattoni's heart was already focused on going back south. However, Trapattoni wouldn't give up so easily, and he let this fact be known: the team started out victorious in the latter part of the season, and Trapattoni and his players took on the challenge of the Champions League with passion and dedication. They reached the semi-finals, achieving great things along the way. The team was weakened by injuries to several players, among them Matthäus, who was out for months with a torn Achilles tendon. They had to play IFK Göteborg for seventy minutes with only ten men, but were able to win the tie on the away-goal rule with any score draw, as the first leg had finished 0–0. As captain Thomas Helmer expressed in his noteworthy, almost melodramatic speech at the banquet after the 2–2 draw, they were also fighting for Trapattoni on this cool March evening in Sweden, since he had 'always stood up for us and was so patient with us'.

Of course, FC Bayern didn't suddenly start playing fantastic football: they didn't always manage to implement Trapattoni's concepts and requirements. After the 1–0 win in the local derby against TSV 1860, the coach did something quite unusual. He apologised to his counterpart Werner Lorant for the victory, saying that it wasn't ability that had given them the win, but rather luck. He earned quite a lot of respect for admitting this.

Trapattoni began to feel the omnipotence of the football 'Kaiser' during these months. Beckenbauer thought that the coach spent too much time concentrating on the European Cup and not enough on the national league. Small, and sometimes larger, jabs were continually communicated through the newspaper or on television, until the accused could no longer remain quiet – and, in fact, had no desire to do so. He challenged the club's boss to 'say what he has to say to my face. I've been a coach for eighteen years, longer than Franz'.

It wasn't a very easy time for Trapattoni. Moreover, shortly before the end of the season, he committed a faux pas that should never have happened. With Bayern 5–2 up against Eintracht Frankfurt, he put on a fourth substitute – even though, according to the rules, only three are allowed. Instead of two points, they got none, and the victory turned into a 0–2 loss. Trapattoni took all the blame, although the manager, Uli Hoeneß, and assistant coach Klaus Augenthaler were also on the bench at the time and failed to keep track of the number of substitutes that had been used. 'It was my oversight,' Trapattoni said. The club then ended up in danger of losing their spot in the UEFA Cup. It was difficult to imagine that Bayern might not be able to play on the European stage in the upcoming season. They had to finish with a good run in the domestic league, or win the Champions League – which was looking unlikely, as they were going up against Ajax Amsterdam, the best team in Europe that year. After a respectable scoreless draw in

Holland against the future Champions League winners, no one held it against them that they weren't able to clear the final hurdle: they lost the second leg 2–5 at home.

After failing to qualify for the finals, it was difficult for the team to motivate themselves for what they had to do on the national level. Trapattoni had little sympathy for that attitude, but he also seemed to have resigned himself to the situation. He remained unfailingly loyal, and would never severely criticise his players publicly. The first Munich interlude did, however, end quite peacefully: FC Bayern spoiled their future coach Otto Rehhagel's final match against Werder Bremen. The Munich players defeated Bremen in the season's final game in the Olympic Stadium, and as a result, Bremen were knocked off the top of the table and surrendered the championship to Borussia Dortmund. This was not a good start for Rehhagel, but it was quite a reasonable farewell for Trapattoni. A couple of weeks after his departure from the club, he admitted: 'I am sorry about my decision to leave FC Bayern, truly very sorry.'

CAGLIARI
1995–1996

Trapattoni's next position would be in Italy once again. Having made his decision in the winter, he now had almost six months to find a new job in Italy, so there was no rush during his last months with FC Bayern. He was able to spend time considering the options back home. Of course, now that he was fifty-six years old, a job as the Italian national coach would be the greatest challenge for him, and maybe even his last. However, in the summer, the European Championships would reach their final stages, and until then nothing would happen. Arrigo Sacchi, who was not beyond criticism, was still in charge and had led Italy to the World Cup finals in 1994. Trapattoni could only hope that Italy wouldn't fulfil expectations in England at Euro '96, but that wasn't his way. He wouldn't wish failure on his colleagues, and he was careful not to arouse suspicion that he was speculating about Sacchi's position. Before the beginning of the finals, he accepted an offer to become the coach of the

Sardinian club US Cagliari for the next season. And everyone knew: Trapattoni keeps his promises.

Although his time with FC Bayern had not really produced the results that he had hoped for – or that he had become accustomed to over the years – it had improved his image in his own country. People thought that he would revive the Italian Serie A, which had recently fallen into extreme financial difficulties. On his return, the *Gazzetta dello Sport* even portrayed him as the deliverer of hope for a languishing league. 'Trapattoni's providence and his eternal enthusiasm are the only things that will lead us back to the sport's basics, a sport that is on its deathbed,' wrote the sport newspaper, which dramatically portrayed Trapattoni as the 'antidote to a football lacking poetry'.

But why Cagliari? Why a team that hadn't played against the best clubs in Italian football for quite a long time? US Cagliari wouldn't play in any European competition in the coming season, and they had no chance against the top teams in Italy. Milan, Inter and Juve are international clubs, whereas Cagliari is a provincial one. For the first time in his career, Trapattoni was leaving the international football stage in order to try his luck with an outsider. And while Sardinia is indeed part of Italy, it was not his homeland, nor that of his wife. Milan and Rome are far away. His family did not join him in Cagliari: Paola and Alberto, his son, remained in Milan. He certainly could have earned more somewhere else, because although many clubs in Italy were in debt, there was no noticeable move to economise. Regardless, it had never been about money for Trapattoni. Perhaps becoming league champions was exactly what he was craving after the sometimes Hollywood-like spectacle he had experienced with FC Bayern.

There were no stars on the Cagliari team; in fact, there were only eighteen players in the squad. The striker Ricardo Oliveira, a Brazilian with a Belgian passport, was the best player, but he hadn't played against the stars on the international stage. Trapattoni wouldn't be Trapattoni if this rather underwhelming situation had prompted him to lower his standards: he wanted success, whether he was training an international club or a placid island club. At the signing of his contract, he promised Cagliari UEFA Cup qualification by the following season, but he soon had to accept the fact that the players just weren't in that category. Trapattoni saw his objective extending far into the future, pushed into the almost unreachable distance: the team was lagging behind from the start. Moreover, they had even slipped down into the relegation zone.

Trapattoni got a visit from Germany in January. The Bayern team and their new coach, Otto Rehhagel, had decided to use Sardinia as their winter training location. Of course, Trapattoni happily helped them with their organisation; he invited his former players and his successor, together with their back-room team, to a restaurant specialising in Sardinian dishes. It was obvious how good he felt to be back in his old circles. Munich's manager, Uli Hoeneß, brought all kinds of Bavarian delicacies, like wheat beer and sausages – delicious treats that Trapattoni had learnt to appreciate during his short time in Munich. In a friendly game against Bayern,

Trapattoni's team managed a respectable 2–2 draw.

The Italian had not forgotten Munich, Bayern and Germany. He still drove an Opel, Bayern's sponsor's car, kept in contact with his former players from Munich, and continued to take German lessons. He said that he would happily come back to Germany if he was asked. At this point, it was already certain that he would not spend another season in Sardinia. He started discussions with AS Roma in February, and there were even rumours that he had already agreed to a three-year contract with the club's president, Franco Sensi. It never got to that point, however. A couple of days later, he resigned as US Cagliari's coach. He was probably anticipating being fired as coach for the first time in his career. After a 1–4 loss to Juventus, who were in fourth place in the table, Cagliari were thirteenth in the league. There wasn't much left to the Sardinian adventure, which had seemed like a good idea at the beginning. However, with 322 wins, Trapattoni was at least getting inexorably closer to Nereo Rocco's record of 326 wins as a Serie A coach.

Bayern Munich, Part II
1996–1998

Giovanni Trapattoni's withdrawal from Cagliari came just at the right time for FC Bayern Munich. The champions were no longer especially fond of Otto Rehhagel – or rather, more to the point, they had quickly developed 'issues' with the new coach.

The switch from Trapattoni to Rehhagel ten months earlier was like a culture shock for the team as well as those in charge. Rehhagel, originally a painter from Essen, had indeed enjoyed a lot of success with Werder Bremen in his fourteen years there. Nevertheless, he wasn't used to working with an entire ensemble of star players and within a media environment that was ill-disposed towards him from the beginning. Moreover, he had to take on a leadership role for the first time in a situation where he was confronted with an impressive accumulation of footballing expertise. Rehhagel incorrectly believed that he could be as autocratic with the players in Munich as he had been with those in Bremen. He emerged as a close-minded, communication-shy coach – the extreme opposite of Trapattoni, the world-travelled coach who always had time to listen to his players.

Sometimes you only fully appreciate what you had once it's gone. When FC Bayern's executives had to come to terms with the fact that the unharmonious relationship between the team and the coach was no longer repairable, they asked Trapattoni if he would consider coming back to Munich if necessary.

Trapattoni could. He had already started to regret his decision of the previous summer. The fact that Bayern had contacted their former coach wasn't kept a secret for long. However, Trapattoni, always the gentleman, didn't want to say much about it. 'I know what it is like when you are under pressure and they're already talking about a successor.'

When Bayern lost yet another home game – 0–1 to Hansa Rostock – those responsible realised that they had to deal with the situation immediately. They saw that it wasn't just the championship that was in danger, but also the impending UEFA Cup final against Bordeaux. The Munich executives discussed appointing Trapattoni right away as the new coach, but that would not be a good new beginning for the Italian. He wouldn't be able to effect much change so quickly, even though he knew most of the players. Beckenbauer took over so that, if something went wrong, Trapattoni wouldn't be resented for it too much. In the event, things didn't go too badly. FC Bayern did indeed lose the league, but they won the UEFA Cup – the only title that they hadn't counted among their collection of trophies so far.

Trapattoni returned to Munich for the first leg against Bordeaux as a guest spectator with his wife Paola. He was met by people who wanted to shake his hands wherever he went throughout the Olympic Stadium. Trapattoni had left barely a year before, and everyone was happy that he would soon be back. All of a sudden, there was a much different and better feeling in both the the team and the club as a whole. 'I began my work here and I would like to finish it.'

He used the weeks before the season began to improve his German and, with the help of the club management, to build up his future team. This team was different from his previous one in that a couple of experienced players had been added and the younger players had matured. He didn't want any new stars but he did want to stop any more desertions from the team. Not everything turned out as he wanted. Andreas Herzog, Jean-Pierre Papin and Ciriaco Sforza could not be dissuaded, and they left the club. Trapattoni was, however, instrumental in signing Ruggiero Rizzitelli, the first Italian professional to move to the German national league. Bayern also enlisted Mario Basler from Werder Bremen. Basler was indeed a genius with the ball, but he was certainly not an exceptional runner or dedicated when it came to training.

Trapattoni showed up promptly for the first practice session but entered through the wrong changing-room door on Säbener Street. Nevertheless, he quickly found his way around his new (or old) environment. He was definitely not the same Trapattoni who had made his debut at FC Bayern two years earlier. Back then, every word had to be translated for him. This time, the translator was still at his side, but the *Signore* only needed his help for an occasional query. He spoke German, if not perfectly, then well enough that the language barrier was gone. 'Now I will be 100 percent Trapattoni.'

Much was the same as it had been during his first spell there at Bayern, notably his coaching style. For that reason, the young players were especially happy that Trapattoni had returned. Rehhagel had not taken an interest in them. He had let it be known through the club management that he had no time for them. In contrast, Trapattoni made time for them. There were once again special sessions after the official practice, especially for the young talent. But there were also some drills, like the double pass, that even the established players had to practise over and over. He justified his theory by stating that 'even Pavarotti has to practise singing every day'.

There was not a great difference between young and old for Trapattoni. He treated them all the same, whether they were national players, world champions or just arrived from an amateur team. In that way, he was able to prevent widespread envy and resentment within the team. In contrast to his predecessor, Rehhagel, he knew how to handle an ensemble of star players, and quickly enjoyed the respect of the players once more. Even the conflict between Jürgen Klinsmann and Lothar Matthäus, who had been ousted from the national team, seemed to have been resolved. They had managed to work things out between them.

Unlike his first season with Bayern, Trapattoni now had an internationally experienced and mature team at his disposal. Two warhorses, Thomas Helmer and Lothar Matthäus, were in defence, as well as Markus Babbel and Christian Ziege, younger but fresh from the European Championship. The young players did indeed dominate the midfield as the newly signed Basler had been injured. However, Dietmar Hamann and Christian Nerlinger were no longer novices in the business; they had already accumulated some merits of their own. Up front, Jürgen Klinsmann had finally found a renowned strike partner in the form of Ruggiero Rizzitelli. The latter was not only a goal-getter but also an excellent passer, endowed with a good eye for his fellow players. Trapattoni saw that the time was ripe to try out the back four, and he extracted the highest level of commitment from the players. As he said: 'The players have to understand: FC Bayern is not a bicycle, it is a Ferrari.'

Everything went well initially. FC Bayern seemed to be growing together. The first round of the cup, against an amateur club, was not the stumbling block this time that it had been two years earlier. The start of the season was also successful. But of course the team was not immune from setbacks, and the UEFA Cup was a good example of this. In the first round, they lost 0–3 to FC Valencia; they were unable to make up the deficit back home in the second leg. The title defenders were already out of the running for a European trophy by the autumn.

Sometimes, it may have seemed as though things were going a little too well. Perhaps the team already assumed that they had achieved their goals. It was at this point that the Munich players came to see another side to the nice *Signore*. When they fell behind in the second half of the away game with Schalke 04, his Italian temperament ran away with him during the half-time break. Trapattoni yelled at the players, and not at all in his usual gentlemanly way. The stewards by the door felt as though the walls throughout the entire stadium were shaking. 'Sometimes one has to get a bit louder.'

Bayern weren't playing as well as the demanding executives had expected. However, there was an increasing degree of organisation in their performance; the defence had finally understood Trapattoni's system. The team conceded fewer goals than anyone else in the national league. Perhaps this was also due to the fact that the experiment of using a back four soon came to an end and they reverted to a sweeper defence.

A problem that the coach had already perceived two years earlier was once again emerging, however: egotism. 'We have a lot of good players, but when they are only playing for themselves, that's not a team.' There were constant complaints from highly paid professionals about substitutions; the loudest of these complaints came from Jürgen Klinsmann, who claimed that he should receive special treatment. The German national striker would also like to have had more order at the front instead of in defence. He still found that FC Bayern didn't play an attacking enough game and that he got too little of the ball. Klinsmann had already complained about Trapattoni's methods and system when he was with Inter.

Bayern won the League Cup in the autumn, losing only one game in the preliminary round. However, the expectations were so high, and their trophy status didn't protect them for long. Moreover, rumours coming out of

Italy that Trapattoni would take over the national team the following summer were also disturbing the coach's work. 'I want to stay with Bayern and nothing else.' Later, AS Roma began to woo Trapattoni; their offer was, without a doubt, tempting to him, but Bayern refused to release him from his contract. For this reason, the approach was quickly settled. This was no real problem for him, since he wanted to finish his work in Munich anyway.

He took the view that there was still much work to be done, and asserted that a lack of communication was the reason for the team's coordination problems and lethargy on the field. 'We have a team with eleven fish,' he said. The second half of the season had its ups and downs. Sometimes the players did a better job in terms of how they communicated and how they played; sometimes a worse one. In the cup competition, the club was eliminated in the quarter-finals against Karlsruhe, but they strove to win the league. The nagging jabs from the executives, above all from Franz Beckenbauer, as well as internal differences, continued to break Trapattoni's focus on winning the title.

Klinsmann's dissatisfaction peaked during the game against SC Freiburg. When the striker didn't follow the coach's instructions and was substituted for the twelfth time that season, he intimated, with an unambiguous hand signal, that he was *finito*: he was finished playing with FC Bayern. After that, he kicked a rubbish bin next to the coach's bench so forcefully that he broke a hole in the thin wood. The kick went down in the annals of football history, and the player would forever be confronted with it. However, Klinsmann was smart enough to know that he was only hurting himself by reacting in such a way: he therefore apologised to Trapattoni at the end of the game. In that way, it was possible that his time working in Munich could come to a peaceful end. One game before the end of the season, Bayern secured the title, and at last the coach was once again highly esteemed in Munich. 'If only everyone was as committed as Trapattoni, we would have become champions with a twenty-point lead,' said Bayer's main critic, Franz Beckenbauer, during the celebrations. Trapattoni was finally able to go where he had wanted to stand two years earlier: on the balcony of Munich's city hall, where the team traditionally parade the trophy for the fans. He then belted out Italian songs in Bavarian dress, finally relaxed, and free from the pressure to succeed.

He received a huge picture from the team with the footprints and signatures of his players. He later hung it up in the small office in his friend's auto-repair shop near Milan, right next to the jerseys of former players like Pelé, Johan Cruyff and Eusébio.

Bayern's record that season was impressive: they were at the top of the table eighteen times, they conceded fewer goals than anyone else, and only two clubs had scored more goals than them – and all this under a coach who was often described as being too slow to attack. As many in FC Bayern had seen throughout the season, he wasn't all that bad. But expectations exceeded even these results. For years, the fans and the higher-ups in the club had been lusting after a team that would thrill the spectators; now, it seemed, they had one.

The eighteenth title in Trapattoni's coaching career was also a victory over himself. In his second year with FC Bayern, he had changed from the kind father figure into a person who could sometimes be seen as a tough old dog. The first time he worked in Munich, he was easy-going – sometimes too much so – and he had now changed that. He had had to recognise that his subtle approach would inevitably fail to work with a collection of egotistical stars. It was clear to him that he would only be able to earn their lasting respect by maintaining a more authoritarian style of leadership. 'Sometimes the dad has to get strict,' he declared. He didn't bother himself much with criticisms of his transfer record, which was incomprehensible for many people. He stuck unwaveringly to his tactics and the team often played successfully, if not always well.

The season ended as Trapattoni had wished, but he had barely recovered from the championship celebrations when he had to put out another fire. Lothar Matthäus, his captain, engaged writers and published his diary, including the locker-room talk at FC Bayern. This was of course not well received by the club. The coach and the management stripped the sweeper of the captain's armband. Trapattoni distanced himself from his 'favourite player' and would not have been disappointed if Matthäus had followed through on his threat to leave the club. With his good contacts with the tabloids and his marked need to tell his story, as he saw it, Matthäus had already manoeuvred himself into an offside position.

Trapattoni now had the worry that if this loose-tongued pro remained on the team, it might cause long-

lasting conflicts that would damage the working atmosphere at the club and endanger the team's success. But
Mätthaus, a World Cup winner, had an influential advocate in Franz Beckenbauer and was allowed to stay.
Trapattoni had to see to it that the outcast was once more
integrated into the team. This seemed to go successfully
for him: Matthäus acted like a model pro. He no longer
called for special privileges, and was unusually tight-
lipped outside the club. In the end, he truly became one
of the many.

The 1997 title win did not challenge Trapattoni publicly to aim for higher goals. The club's executives were
similarly reserved: they were all in agreement that they
had to win the league title again the following season, and
perhaps reach the knockout stages of the Champions
League. At any rate, Trapattoni thought that the team,
under new captain Thomas Helmer, was doing better
than ever before. The champions had been strengthened
for the Maestro's third year: Giovane Elber from VfB
Stuttgart took over Jürgen Klinsmann's position as striker, and the French international Bixente Lizarazu
replaced Christian Ziege on the left side. (The latter had
been sold to AC Milan.) Two players from Karlsruhe,
Michael Tarnat and Thorsten Fink, were in midfield,
where they were more responsible for doing the dirty
work that needed to be done than for any creative playing. In addition, there was a new assistant coach: the club
put gentle pressure on Klaus Augenthaler, Trapattoni's
seasoned assistant from the last two years with Bayern, to
find work elsewhere. He was replaced by Egon Coordes.
Coordes was already under contract in Munich and was

notorious for his sweat-inducing training sessions.

The beginning of the new season wasn't going as well as desired. The promoted team, FC Kaiserslautern, under Trapattoni's predecessor Rehhagel, won 1–0 in Munich. Bayern's first win didn't come until their third match, when they beat Wolfsburg 5–2. This win was, however, representative of the Maestro's new attack-oriented style. The strikers shone, with entrancing short passing, and this allowed the team to hope for many goals that season.

Sometimes, FC Bayern's football was truly thrilling. For example, there were a couple of performances in the reorganised Champions League – with the field extended beyond the champions of the best European leagues. The Munich players beat Paris St Germain in a home game 5–1, but they benefited from the fact that the French played much too openly against the German champions. When Trapattoni was talking about his team's performance in this match, he declared that the music goes 'Ding, dong, dang, not just ding'. However, Trapattoni was continuously reproached for having his team play too carefully: it was said that he put safety ahead of beauty. Trapattoni didn't differentiate between defence and attack; for him, success was all that mattered. The higher-ups had to accept the fact that there wasn't going to be an enjoyable football game every week, especially not when their opponents entrenched themselves in their own penalty box. FC Bayern found it difficult to probe against teams that defended deep in this way.

Trapattoni found, however, that he had a happy football marriage with FC Bayern, and minor frictions are part of the deal in any fulfilling partnership. He extended his contract to 30 June 2000 without, as the vice-president Karl-Heinz Rummenigge assured the media, a release clause for the Italian national team. The Bayern team were on the right track, even though they couldn't get past the surprisingly strong FC Kaiserlautern, who were now top of the national league. Even after the winter break, Bayern lagged behind. They had, however, achieved their goal in international competitions. They had ended top of the table in the group stage of the Champions League and would now face Borussia Dortmund in the quarter-finals – a team who had qualified as runners-up the previous year. Moreover, Trapattoni had once more succeeded in integrating a young player into the team. Carsten Jancker had come to Munich the year before from Rapid Vienna and had achieved a breakthrough during the second season, after many individual sessions with the coach.

Trapattoni developed more and more into an entertainer during his third year at Bayern. Press conferences were quite amusing affairs. Previously, he had almost always appeared with a translator, whereas now he had become his own translator. He would show up with a cheat sheet, on which he had written all the most important phrases and words. He would begin by reading but would then forget what his idea was, and would begin to shift quickly back and forth between Italian and German. Once, he spoke of the 'three beautiful girls' he would like to have: the Championship, the DFB Cup and the Champions League. Another time, Lothar Matthäus revealed Trapattoni's home remedy against getting a cold: 'An espresso in the morning, a wheat beer in the evening.' The coach also sent his greetings out to his alleged legions of female fans on Brazilian television, the land of the world champions: he would beam out at them with his blue eyes.

On the outside, Trapattoni appeared to be in a very good mood; however, he was already beginning to brood. It had been bothering him for a long time that there was a lack of mutual respect between the players in Germany. 'There are too many disputes,' he noted. The situation worsened during the second half of the season. His impression was that the pros were more interested in who received the permanent positions and what their salaries were, rather than in the game of football.

He also now realised that he wasn't immune from being criticised by his players. He wasn't used to this. In Italy, a player would never criticise his coach with impunity in the presence of journalists: there was a code of honour that stated 'Never say something in public about your coach'. Whoever did so would end up on the bench. In Italy, the football club was like a family: the club's decisions were accepted without contradiction. Players were used to conforming, at least outwardly; in return, the coach always defended his players to the media. He had been sticking to this model in Munich as well. However, this model was not always followed by his players. Trapattoni learnt that it was rumoured that his players' loyalty was dwindling. And after the team's third consecutive loss, 0–1 against Schalke 04, Mario Basler, Thomas Strunz and Mehmet Scholl openly blamed the coach's substitution tactics for the first time. It was at this point that Trapattoni had had enough of being patient and friendly.

Two days later, on 10 March 1998, Trapattoni called a press conference for that afternoon. Everything was well prepared. At noon, he called the host of his favourite bar in Munich. 'He said: "Fausto, look at the papers tomorrow, you're going to be surprised at what you see",' the aforementioned Fausto later admitted. At the press conference, Trapattoni appeared, as usual, with a piece of paper, but he only read off slogans from it. Trapattoni created a multilingual memorial for himself with the speech he made that day:

> Now in this team, there are, oh, some players forget professionals they are. I don't read very many newspapers, but I have heard many reports: we have not played offensive. There is no German team plays offensive and the name offensive, like Bayern. Last game we had three strikers: Elber, Jancker and then Zickler. We have to forget Zickler. Zickler is a striker more Mehmet and more Basler. Is clear these words, is possible understand, what I said have? Thank you. Offensive, offensive is like doing on the field.
>
> I explained with these two players: after Dortmund we need maybe half-time pause. I also saw other teams in Europe after this Wednesday. I saw also two days the practice. A coach is not an idiot! A coach see what happen on field. In this game it were two, three or four players, they were weak like a bottle empty!

Have you seen Wednesday what team has played Wednesday? Has played Mehmet or has played Basler or has played Trapattoni? These players complain more than they play.

You know why Italian team not buy these players? Because have seen many times to game. Have said these not play for the Italian championses.

Strunz! Strunz is two years here, has played ten games. Is always injured. What dare Strunz?!

Last year became champions with Hamann, Nerlinger. These players were players! And have become champion. Is always injured. Has played twenty-five game in this team.

Must respect the other colleagues. Have many nice colleagues. Ask the colleagues the question!

I am tired now the father of these players and defend these players. I have always the blame. Over these players. One is Mario the one the other is Mehmet.

Strunz I don't mention, has only played 25 percent of the game.

I have through.

It was an attempt to shake up the team with a view to knocking FC Kaiserslautern off the top of the table. The Bayern executives supported the coach and imposed a fine on the concerned players, as is common practice in Italy. Franz Beckenbauer also read the team the riot act.

A couple of days later, Trapattoni's anger had hardly subsided when he called another meeting of the players and the assistant coach. 'Our team is not broken,' he declared before the second leg of the quarter-finals of the Champions League against Borussia Dortmund.

Prior to this, voices had been raised, accusing Egon Coordes of training the players too hard. They claimed that, as a result, they were weakened for the final stretch of the season and were unable to perform for the full ninety minutes. It was indeed true that the Bayern team dragged their feet around the field more than they ran. It was also suggested, though, that this had more to do with a lack of motivation than overtraining. In Dortmund, they had to play for 120 minutes, and they ended up losing the contest with their league rivals. Trapattoni was deeply affected by the defeat; he didn't show up at the official meal, perhaps as a silent commentary on the events of the previous week. He recognised that the top-quality players in the squad would never work with him in the way he wanted them to – and in the way he was used to. He recognised that he wasn't going to be able to get anything else out of this team and that only major change would bring about improvement. However, he realised that he wasn't sure that he wanted to be the one to carry out the required reorganisation.

Moreover, support for Trapattoni as manager was waning. Franz Beckenbauer praised at length Dortmund's sport's director and former coach, Ottmar Hitzfield. Bayern vice-president Karl-Heinz Rummenigge declared that Trapattoni was a 'persona grattissima', but he seemed to be the only one of the executives who was seriously interested in continuing to work with him. Bayern, who held the record for the number of domestic titles won, had increasing worries that they were also going to lose their second place, which they needed to maintain in order to be able to qualify for the Champions League the following season. There was one last chance to save the season: the DFB Cup. The Bayern team were at least able to reach the finals there, for the first time in twelve years.

Trapattoni resignedly laid the contract which had been signed just a couple months earlier on manager Ulli Hoeneß's desk and asked to be released from it at the end of the domestic season. The Italian newpapers soon quoted the Maestro as saying: 'I'm coming back [to Italy] at the end of the season.' However, in Germany, the public would only be informed about Trapattoni's impending move at the end of the derby against the TSV 1860 Munich.

The press conference after the game was, as always, shown on the screen in the Olympic Stadium. Many fans were waiting there since it had been leaked that an announcement would be made about something that everyone had already suspected. As the president, Franz Beckenbauer, expressed his regrets over Trapattoni's departure, there were whistles – more whistles, in fact, than this guiding light of German football had ever heard. Trapattoni was the only one to receive any applause; the spectators had a keen sense of the poor way in which the Bayern executives had treated Trapattoni. Bayern's attempt to explain the change of coaches in an elegant fashion misfired. Trapattoni tried everything to show the club in a good light, and claimed that there had been 'many small reasons' for his departure, among them the language barrier – a barrier that for a long time had, in truth, barely existed. FC Bayern's fans were not always in agreement about how the Bayern players had performed under Trapattoni. However, they valued the Italian's genteel style and good manners, and such things also count in football.

The public provided Trapattoni with a quiet farewell for what would be his last German national league game – at least for the time being. Even the players, who had sometimes let him down badly, made one last effort for the Signore. Despite a 4–0 win against Borussia Dortmund, they didn't have enough points for the title – although, if truth be told, after the trials and tribulations of the last few weeks, no one at FC Bayern had expected this. Trapattoni had been Bayern's head coach for 102 German national league games; the hard-working helpers in the stadium recounted that, after every game, they would find the black-and-white wrappers of his favourite Milan caramel next to the coach's bench.

Trapattoni wasn't quite finished in Munich. The last trip he made with Bayern was to Berlin, to the cup final. The team beat MSV Duisburg 2–1 there and bestowed one more title on the coach – even if, for him as well as the club, this cup was the least important of the 'three ladies'.

Before handing over the cup, Bayern's main sponsor showed a short film about Trapattoni on the Berlin Olympic Stadium's big screen. At the end of the film, as homage to Trapattoni, the narrator said: 'He was our partner and will remain our friend.'

FIORENTINA

1998–2000

Trapattoni's knowledge of German was improving, but he was still limited linguistically. Although in the autumn of 1997 he extended his contract with Bayern Munich until 2000, he let it be known in April 1998 that he was leaving. His 'I have through' speech had been aired about a month earlier, and perhaps he had also been hurt by the ridiculing of his remarks, begun by the late-night TV host Harald Schmidt.

So where should a sixty-year-old football coach who, even after having enjoyed immense success, was still deemed to be an advocate for a pragmatic, defence-oriented style, go now? Was Giovanni Trapattoni just an obsolete model that should go into retirement?

There could be no discussion of retirement. Trapattoni knew the meaning of the word 'work' because of the example his parents had set for him. Vittorio Cecchi-Gori, a film-maker and a massive football fan, offered him a job that was more suitable for someone who wanted to commit suicide rather than for someone who made their living in football: that of the coach of AC Fiorentina. The fans of the 'Purples' from Florence were among the most demanding in Italian football. The team had to play to win, and play beautifully. And watch out if they didn't!

Trapattoni loves Tuscany. For the previous thirty-five years, he had spent his holidays in Talamone, a picturesque little village on the coast in the Grosseto province. This village, which is 160 kilometres from Rome, is known as the historical residence of the freedom fighter Giuseppe Garibaldi, who stopped in Talamone during his 'Expedition of the Thousand'. For Trapattoni, its significance lay in the fact that his daughter Alessandra had met her future husband, Jacopo, a Florentine, there.

Trapattoni agreed to take up the job in Florence and started it with the same aim he had with all his previous coaching jobs: to leave his imprint on the team, to let it be known that he had had an effect there. He was warmly welcomed to the city. The club chairman and the media received hundreds of letters and faxes, in which the fans waxed poetic about his appointment: 'You are a wish that has no memory, like a hope that has no boundaries. On this day, you show yourself as the light in every mirror, after an eternity of waiting. We don't see it yet, but we are enthusiastically following your every step.' Another *tifoso* (fan) wrote: 'Before you even win on the field, you are able to win the hearts of every person you meet. You are also the "Trap", even when the ball doesn't make it into every goal, as you would wish it to.' Others remembered an incident that had taken place years before, when

Trapattoni was with Inter Milan in Naples. Some fans wanted to get an autograph from him, but it was 9 PM, and the coach was already in his room, probably in his pyjamas. He was called on his phone and, ten minutes later, was standing in the lobby: 'Good evening to you all, I am sorry I am not wearing a tie.'

Trapattoni's years of success with rivals Juventus were forgiven in Florence. For years, his image was equated with Juventus's image of power, arrogance and invincibility. Now, however, the fans were discovering that this man, who in the past had whistled and screamed and ranted for Turin, now whistled and screamed and ranted for their team. They recognised that their world-weariness at the time was not God-given, but rather homemade. 'Keep doing what you're doing. You're going to change Florence, and that's not easy,' the fans would say to him, recommending that he dye his hair purple. They described him as the most wonderful experience since AC Fiorentina came into existence, and celebrated the 'Trap storm'.

Trapattoni accomplished the impossible and reignited Florence's not-quite-extinguished football fever. In fact, he started an inferno. In October 1998, Fiorentina headed the championship table. The club had 2,800 tickets available for the UEFA Cup game against Grasshoppers Zürich, and could have sold twice as many.

It was a season *da incorniciare* – to be treasured. In the end, the Tuscan team finished third in Serie A, qualifying them for participation in the Champions League. Club management and the players, who included the Argentinian legend Gabriel Batistuta, and the fans were so pleased with Trapattoni's work that Fiorentina's patron Cecchi-Gori offered him a 'lifetime contract'. 'I want him to be bound to the club for life,' said the film producer.

But football is a fast-moving business. A year later, there was no longer any talk of the lifetime contract; quite the opposite, in fact. Believing that they lacked discipline and desire, Trapattoni was extremely hard on his players during training. The results were extremely slow in coming; Trapattoni, fair and consistent as ever, offered to step down in 1999. This offer was not accepted, but his departure from the club was only delayed. At the beginning of 2000, the fans, who had previously given him loud applause, reacted to the lean results by boycotting a cup game. Trapattoni was the scapegoat: the Florentines did indeed get to the knockout stage of the Champions League, but the coach had had enough. He left. He would be quoted as saying that being a coach in Florence is harder than reaching the top of Mount Everest. He didn't want to deal with the hostile reactions from the fans any more.

THE ITALIAN NATIONAL TEAM
2000–2004

For Trapattoni, football was about mistakes. Whoever makes the fewest mistakes, wins. An average performance ending in a draw is better than a loss with flying colours. His work in the larger clubs with the big-name players had affected him as both a coach and a man. He didn't see himself as a tough-as-nails coach or a dictator, but rather loved the dialogue with the team. He demanded two things of his players: discipline, both on and off the field, and social equality. No one should feel as though they are inferior to anyone else. He refused to be dictated to by anyone in his work. As an employee of the club, he saw himself as partly responsible for protecting the club's financial assets. This factor was more important to him than the implementation of new football theories.

Trapattoni became the Italian national team's coach a few days after Italy lost the final of Euro 2000 to France, 1–2, in extra time. There had been frequent discussions about him taking the position of national coach, but it had never been the right time for him to make the move. Now, in the summer of 2000, there was indeed a happy ending: Trapattoni and the Italian football association came together. Somewhat surprisingly, Dino Zoff had resigned his position as Italian coach after the team's final loss at Euro 2000. Formerly the Italian team's first-choice goalkeeper, he had taken over Cesare Maldini's job after Italy's defeat in the quarter-finals of the 1998 World Cup. However, it wasn't Italy's defeat in the final that was given as Zoff's reason for leaving, but rather the strong criticism by Silvio Berlusconi of Zoff's management of the national team.

Zoff was indeed deemed to be *the* expert on football, but he wasn't media-friendly. The Italian reporters called him 'the mummy' because he would always stand on the sidelines with the same stony-faced expression, regardless of whether the team won or lost. Zoff didn't talk much, and when he did, he gave little indication of being either pleased or disappointed. 'Dino Nazionale', as he was known, wasn't able to sell himself well – somthing that may have played a part in his eventual downfall. The Italian opposition leader, Silvio Berlusconi, branded Zoff a dilettante. The national coach took this as an assault on his honour and quickly resigned. Despite numerous attempts by the club's functionaries to change his mind, he stuck to his decision.

The search for a successor to Zoff proved to be fairly straightforward. In the past, Trapattoni had always been deemed a promising candidate for the position, but he had always had other commitments. Now, however, he had just ended his employment with Fiorentina and he was not talking to anybody else yet. It was reported that he was going to succeed Erich Ribbeck at Bayern Leverkusen, but it became clear that this rumour was without foundation.

Trapattoni spent eaerly July at his house in Talamone. There he could skip his morning run, drink coffee with the neighbours, and talk to the journalists who regularly besieged him, asking him whether there was any news. 'I don't know anything about anything,' he told them. 'I am not a psychic.' He also learnt more German and repaired his satellite dish in order not to miss any of the matches he might want to watch.

Talamone is a simple, no-nonsense sort of a place. He sat with friends – and bit his lip when they told him that he should remain quiet because he didn't understand anything about football. Here, he sang folk songs, had barbecues until the early hours and sipped his 'apéritif di Calía', made from orange juice, gin, Campari and lemon. Here, he finally shook off the media.

Around noon on 6 July, he set out for Rome to conclude the talks on the position of national coach. His wife Paola stalled the journalists, who were looking for him. Initially, she told them: 'He's resting right now.' Later, she came out with the truth: 'Oh, sorry to see you waiting. Giovanni is in Rome.' After 6 PM, Paola asked the journalists: 'Are you still here? Giovanni is still in Rome.' 'We know, we know,' they replied. 'As of a few minutes ago, he's the new national team coach. It's official.' The new first lady of Italian football rolled her eyes. 'Oh really? He signed? He hasn't called me yet. It will be the pinnacle of his career.' And with that, she looked up to the sky with a sigh and said: '*Speriamo che Dio gliela mandi buoni*' – 'May God be with him.'

His friends in Talamone were happy that he was going to become the coach of the Italian national team rather than that of the German team. They said that the German players were too clumsy for Trapattoni: 'They just stand in their positions, and if the ball rolls a metre away from their spot, they don't move to get it. The Italians, yes, they are completely different. And the communication would finally work well. A whistle from the bench, and everyone would know exactly what he was supposed to do.'

For Luciano Nizzola, the head of the Italian football assocation, Trapattoni was a 'born winner' who was the ideal combination of an intelligent tactician and a glamorous media man. There were virtually no other coaches who appeared so often – and so charmingly – in front of the public. He had always cultivated a friendly relationship with the journalists, seeing them as partners rather than opponents, and always trying to maintain a businesslike relationship with them. This approach definitely helped when the performance on the field didn't live up to expectations. Consequently, the newspapers were full of praise for the signing. 'It is like voting for a pope that everybody agrees on,' the *Gazetta dello Sport* editorialised. There were certainly a couple of small reservations about Trapattoni's appointment, however, as he wasn't especially known for bold, attacking football. His signing was therefore an indication that Italy were unlikely to change their style of playing.

There were two particularly attractive aspects to Trapattoni: on the one hand, his passion, his almost childlike excitement, and on the other, his way of expressing himself, both non-verbally and verbally. Whoever believed that the coach only had an eccentric speaking style in German was wrong. His temper also ran away with him in his mother tongue – sometimes to such an extent that he ended up creating funny Italian constructions or completely new expressions. A couple of weeks after the announcement of his appointment as the national coach, the Roman university La Sapienza went to see him in order to study his mode of expression.

The reaction to Trapattoni's employment as the new national coach turned out to be as positive as might have been expected. Perhaps it was because he was old and had a face that everyone found to be friendly.

'I'm happy for him; I wish him all the best. Advice? I never give advice to anyone,' said his predecessor, Dino Zoff. Alessandro Altobelli, who had met Trapattoni during his time at Inter Milan, commented on the signing by referring to the fact that it had always been Trapattoni's dream to have the head-coach job: 'He has great charisma, he's the right coach.' Vittorio Cecchi-Gori saw that his views were confirmed and addressed himself to the Fiorentina fans who had cast the Maestro out of Tuscany, saying: 'His call to this position is also an answer to every *tifoso* who didn't understand him well enough and didn't appreciate him.' And Arrigo Sacchi, a coach in the 1990s, said: 'He's the right man on the right stage. I wish him the success and fulfilment that he has earned.'

Now, one could say, somewhat ironically – and somewhat cynically, perhaps – that Sacchi was very polite when Trapattoni was appointed. Sacchi and Trapattoni are not friends, because they have intrinsically different views about football tactics. The right man on the right stage? A defensive expert who relished the memories of the *catenaccio* of the 1960s. The right one for the leadership of the national team, the highest expression of the country's footballing art? I beg your pardon? Had Sacchi been converted? Was he betraying his innovative zonal-defence approach, which had provided him with so much success? Had he forgotten what Trapattoni had said years earlier? That true football wasn't about theory and that he would still choose Fabio Capello over Arrigo Sacchi? That he, Sacchi, had lost three out of the four championship titles but that his playing system had been praised to the heavens due to a propaganda machine? That the term 'zonal defence' and 'pressing' had come from basketball and that they are defensive tactics? That the national team had only played well in five games with Sacchi? Sacchi versus Trapattoni – that was a contest like the one from the Italian professional cycling world: Gino Bartali versus Fausto Coppi. Trapattoni could only smile about it and say: 'I'm Bartali. He was older than Coppi, and I'm older than Sacchi.'

SEASON	ARRIGO SACCHI WITH AC MILAN	GIOVANNI TRAPATTONI WITH INTER MILAN
GOALS (FOR–AGAINST)		
1987/88	43–14	42–35
1988/89	61–25	67–19
1989/90	56–27	55–32
1990/91	46–19	56–31
TOTAL	206–85	220–117
SCORELESS DRAWS		
1987/88	11 (6)	10 (0)
1988/89	14 (7)	6 (3)
1989/90	5 (2)	10 (5)
1990/91	10 (3)	10 (3)
TOTAL	40 (18)	36 (11)

Source: *La Gazzetta dello Sport* (29 November 1995)

Whatever about the record books, the right man on the right stage was Giovanni Trapattoni. He was a man who could make himself understood even by a group of Japanese with his gestures, as Arrigo Sacchi once said. Trapattoni had talked to the Italian football assocation about the post of Italian head coach repeatedly over the years and it had repeatedly fallen through. He wanted to continue to work with the group of players that Dino Zoff had assembled. He proposed a tactical system of 3–5–2 or 4–4–2, and announced that he wanted to play with two strikers and an additional floating striker.

On 3 September 2000, Trapattoni began his career as the coach of the *Azzurri* with the first qualifying stage for the 2002 World Cup in Japan and South Korea. (The

Italian FA already had plans to replace Trapattoni after 2002 with Marco Tardelli, the coach of the Under 21s, but who knew that at this point?) The national coach's first press conference lasted ninety minutes: the new *commissario tecnico* spoke – or, rather, philosophised – about football. At the end of the press conference, there was a glass of spumante for the journalists, and then Trapattoni stepped on to his training field, beaming like a small child at his first day of school.

In any event, Trapattoni didn't make an ideal debut, with a 2–2 draw against Hungary in Népstadion in Budapest. With the exception of Filippo Inzaghi, the team's 'spearhead' remained lethargic – a problem for an attack-minded outfit. The coach thought that the players' mediocre performance was due to a lack of training: that they were in the middle of preparing for Serie A season, which had yet to begin, and therefore weren't yet in their best condition. The first game was on 7 October, in the San Siro Stadium in Milan – the place where everything had begun for Trapattoni. It was there that he had attended his first AC Milan game in 1954. Then, he had taken public transport and walked four kilometres, taking ninety minutes to get to the ground. He had begun his career as a player and a coach there, had competed with Pelé and Brazil. Before the first home game, he declared: 'Maybe it will end the same with Romania as with Brazil, 3–0.'

And it did. Inzaghi, Marco Delvecchio and Francesco Totti made sure that they achieved the desired result. Trapattoni was true to himself, and continued his lively whistling as national coach. Ernst Happel, one of the top coaches in the world, whistled more than Trapattoni did, and better than him – without the two little fingers that Trapattoni needed. The papers were falling over themselves with praise for the Italian players. He was the greatest, they said. Within just a couple of weeks, Trapattoni had managed to combine the best characteristics of the coach with those of the players. And surprisingly, that didn't mean *catenaccio*, but rather a spectacle – an entrancing game.

Italy beat Georgia three days later in Ancona, 2–0, and on 15 November, in the Delle Alpi Stadium in Turin, the *Azzurri* defeated England in a friendly, 1–0, with Gennaro Gattuso getting the goal. They qualified for the World Cup without losing: in eight games, they had six wins and two draws. (They also won a friendly against England in Leeds on 27 March 2002, 2–1.) Before the Asian tour, the Italian FA extended Trapattoni's contract up to the 2004 World Cup.

Italy were drawn with Ecuador, Croatia and Mexico in the group stage of the World Cup. Of course, the *Azzurri* were favourites to win the group, and of course everybody back home was waiting for them to win all their matches on their way into the last sixteen. Trapattoni had made a very unpopular decision when he named his squad by dropping Roberto Baggio. Baggio had been in spectacular form before his cruciate rupture in February: he had scored eleven goals in twelve games for Brescia, who had just been promoted into Serie A. Italian football supporters and the media demanded that Baggio play, but Trapattoni didn't believe that the thirty-five-year-old would be able to contribute much to the team in the Far East.

Italy's campaign began promisingly, with a 2–0 win against Ecuador. The team was well organised and goal-oriented. They played without too much pomp and ceremony – and nobody missed Baggio. However, in the second game, everything changed when they were stunned by a 1–2 loss to Croatia. Trapattoni even momentarily lost his composure – not because his team was playing so badly, but rather because of the referee, who disallowed two goals, by Christian Vieri and Inzaghi. The controversial decisions annoyed the fans back home as well. The media blamed the loss mainly on the referee. Trapattoni didn't get away completely scot-free, however: he was accused (not for the first time) of not having sent enough strikers on to the pitch.

During the deciding game for entry into the last sixteen, the *commissario tecnico* yielded to the pressure (or maybe he had planned to do it all along) and put Vieri and Inzaghi up front and Totti behind them, in order to have the best chance of winning. Trapattoni left nothing to chance in this game, and made use of everything that could bring him and the team luck. His wife Paola was sitting in the stands, and he had a small bottle of holy water in his jacket pocket. His sister was a nun and had given it to him to take with him to Japan and South Korea. 'Why not?' he asked. 'I also pray before every game.'

He had put a couple of drops of the holy water on his wrist for the game against Croatia, but it had not had the desired effect. Against Mexico, however, it did help. The Central Americans went ahead, but Alessandro del Piero, the striker who had let Trapattoni down at the World Cup, managed to even up the score in the seventy-eighth minute, just before being substituted. Ecuador's victory over Croatians meant that the Italian team's draw was enough for them to finish second in the group and move on to the next round.

On Tuesday 18 June, in Daejeon, Italy played South Korea. The Ecuadorian referee, Byron Moreno, spoiled the game for the 38,558 spectators. The game ended 1–1 after ninety minutes. (Vieri scored after eighteen minutes for Italy; Seol Ki-Hyun equalised after eighty-eight for the South Koreans.) Francesco Totti was sent off after 104 minutes and Ahn Jung-Hwan scored the golden goal, in the 117th minute. Trapattoni whistled his heart out, threw bottles around, and spoke about discrimination and cheating. Goals denied, faulty decisions, yellow and red cards: it was a disaster. Not even the holy water given to him by Sister Romilda could prevent Italy's early departure from the tournament.

The truth about this last-sixteen game was that Totti's sending-off was harsh and that Damiano Tommasi's goal in extra time, which was ruled out for offside, should have stood. It was the fifth goal for the Italians that had been disallowed during this World Cup. Putting to one side the strong criticism of Trapattoni's defence-minded approach, the team failed to capitalise on many of the chances they created. By contrast, four years later, at the World Cup in Germany, everything would go to plan. Italy would take their chances, and the referees wouldn't have anything against the *Azzurri*. In short, the Italians would be the lucky ones in 2006. But in 2002, the *Squadra*

Azzurra had to go home, and all of Italy suspected a conspiracy. Trapattoni had kicked a plexiglas wall, behind which sat the FIFA functionaries. Maybe it was a coincidence; maybe not.

After Italy's early exit, the coach's reputation also suffered in the football-crazy country. However, Trapattoni was not even considering stepping down. 'I am full of excitement about my job,' he said, and started preparing for the next big tournament, Euro 2004, to be held in Portugal two years later.

In the end, Marco Tardelli never took over Trapattoni's position. The Italian FA held on to Trapattoni – temporarily, as far as the public was concerned – and went into the Euro 2004 campaign with him. However, the start of the competition was anything but auspicious. A painstaking 2–0 win in Azerbaijan was followed by a 1–1 draw with Serbia-Montenegro (in Naples) and a 1–2 defeat by Wales (in Cardiff). Trapattoni came under fire in the same way that every other coach who didn't win came under fire. On top of that, the Brazilian World Cup coach, Luis Felipe Scolari, applied for his position.

Even though Scolari was hired shortly afterwards by Portugal, the attacks on Trapattoni were increasing. His team had had only two wins in the last ten games, and the media were portraying him as an out-of-date model. The president of the Italian FA, Franco Carraro, wanted to take a poll among the players, but the players reacted furiously to being asked to make the decision about their coach's future. 'It is a disgrace that we have to give our opinions,' said goalkeeper Gianluigi Buffon. After a two-hour-long meeting in Rome, Trapattoni and the executives of the Italian FA agreed to continue to work together. He was backed up by coaching colleagues, who argued that Trapattoni could only work with those players who were made available to him.

With their backs to the wall, the Italians were praying for a good performance. They beat Finland twice, won a friendly in Stuttgart against Germany 1–0, and secured first place in their group thanks to a 4–0 win against Wales, on 6 September 2003, in Milan (courtesy of a hat-trick from Inzaghi and a goal from Del Piero). In the event, Italy seemed to have qualified easily – and the difficulties along the way were quickly forgotten. Moreover, the Italian clubs' revival in Europe gave the lie to the critique of the national coach: Inter, Milan and Juventus all made it through to the Champions League semi-finals in 2003, mainly by playing organised, safe football à la Trapattoni.

On the other hand, Trapattoni refused to accept the view that his style was too defence-oriented, describing his approach rather as 'attack-minded defence', which forces the opponent to make mistakes. In 2003, Trapattoni's team won seven times in eight competitive and friendly games. The only goal they conceded in these eight games was to Serbia-Montenegro (in a 1–1 draw) at the end of the Euro qualification round.

Trapattoni had hit his stride by the time Euro 2004 began. With three attackers and a very attack-minded Mauro Camoranesi, he was trying to lay to rest, once and for all, his reputation for having too strong a love for a *catenaccio* approach. He played Vieri, although he hadn't had a good season with Inter that year. He also put out Del Piero, even though everyone said that he always failed at the big tournaments. And of course he put Totti out. To the confusion of the entire Italian football world, however, he decided against playing the young Parma forward Alberto Gilardino.

Even before the kick-off, the first signs of resentment about the way in which he had organised the team began to appear. First of all, Gennaro Gattuso, the ankle-biter from AC Milan who was playing as a defensive midfielder, was outraged because he felt as though he had been ignored by Trapattoni. The boss ignored this and let all substitute players know that he expected support from them for their colleagues on the field. Another cause for complaint was the privileged position that Totti held in the team. The Roman was Trapattoni's favourite: in almost all the teams that he had trained, he placed his confidence above all in one player. Totti was the leader of the team, and this wasn't liked by everyone. For example, Del Piero, Stefano Fiore and the rookie Antonio Cassano felt as though they weren't appreciated enough by Trapattoni. This problem was solved quickly – although not in a way that the Italians would have wished. Totti was suspended for three games for spitting on his opponent Christian Paulsen at the start of a game against Denmark – an incident that was picked up by Danish television.

Without Totti, there was more pressure on the rest of the team – including the ones who had complained about the special treatment given to their leader. However, when they ended up with a 1–1 draw with Sweden in the second group match, it wasn't the team but the coach that was attacked. The newspapers were writing that Trapattoni was ruining everything and 'sentencing Italy to death' – even though he had in fact done almost nothing wrong. For an hour, the team had played superbly, and Totti was completely forgotten about. However, they had failed to maintain their lead: Italy had played deeper and deeper, and conceded a goal just before the whistle blew, resulting in a draw.

The scenario before the final group matches couldn't have been worse for the Italians: they were dependent on Denmark and Sweden. If the Scandinavian game ended with a 2–2 draw, Trapattoni's men were out, regardless of how heavily they beat Bulgaria. It ended just as the *Azzurri* had anticipated: the northern Europeans played out a 2–2 draw. The result left some doubts hanging in the air because Sweden scored their equaliser just before the end, and the Danish goalkeeper, Thomas Sorensen, didn't exactly make the most splendid effort to block it. Italy's hard-won 2–1 victory over the already eliminated and therefore unmotivated Bulgarians was secured by a goal by Antonio Cassano in the ninetieth minute. This win didn't placate the critics at home, however. Italy could count themselves amongst the Greats who had been eliminated prematurely, including Germany and England. The *Azzurri* were already on holiday when Greece surprisingly beat Portugal in the finals.

Trapattoni's biggest dream would therefore never come to pass: to end his time as Italian coach with a trophy. He had already given notice that he would step down after the European Championship, and now he wouldn't even be asked if he wanted to continue. His successor had long been chosen: Marcello Lippi. Trapattoni deserved a better send-off than the one he was given in Italy. The media and the public were merciless in their treatment of him and claimed that he had put out the same players who, according to them, had already failed at the World Cup two years before. Nevertheless, Trapattoni left with his head held high. In his opinion, he could not be reproached because he had not lost any matches in Portugal. And despite the fact that they had the same number of points as Denmark and Sweden, they were still eliminated. He was finished in Italy, but he wasn't going to be finished with football for a long time to come.

During his four years as the head of the team, and while implementing his zonal-defence system, Trapattoni learnt that Italian football was very good technically and tactically, and that the players were (or could be) mentally strong. But he had also learnt that Italian football wasn't the best in the world, and certainly not as good as it would like to be. However, now Giovanni Trapattoni's career as national coach was finished – perhaps too quickly, and definitely not with as much success as he might have had. He deserved to have won more: his outstanding coaching career had not been crowned in fitting style. Trapattoni was replaced in June 2004 and once again had to ask himself: what next for the most successful coach in Italy, and one of the most successful coaches in the world?

Trapattoni, the son of a blue-collar worker, knew that football had made him rich. However, his ideals were those of every socialist. When he spends money, he spends it secretly. He is actively involved with the Catholic Church and speaks to young people in schools. But the man from Milan also knows the value of labour. So he didn't sniff at the offer he received from Benfica, and why should he? He had no job and there, on the western edge of Europe, there were some things that had to be taken care of. He could leave his mark there. Lisbon is not Madrid, where Antonio Camacho was going. There wasn't any real work for a coach at Real, just the management of a star team. However, with Benfica, he would once again have daily work on the field, work that he hadn't been able to accomplish as the national coach.

Trapattoni as a player with the Italian national team

Benfica's Eusébio and Trapattoni, of AC Milan, during the 1963 European Cup final at Wembley.

© Votava

The Italian national team c. 1962: Trapattoni is in the front row, third from right. Cesare Maldini, who would also go on to manage Italy, is at the extreme left of the back row.

With Nils Liedholm, who was both a friend to and an influence on Trapattoni.

Trapattoni training Paulo Rossi, who moved to Juventus just after winning the Golden Boot and the Golden Ball as the top goal-scorer in the 1982 World Cup.

'I am Agnelli': a visit by Trapattoni to the Juventus bench

As a workhorse, at the centre of events and (above) brooding before a game

The lonely life of a trainer

Having a quiet word with Aldo Serena, Inter Milan's top goal-scorer when they won the Serie A with Trapattoni in 1989

Great minds think alike: with Löthar Matthäus, his former assistant manager at Salzburg. Matthäus was also a key player for Trapattoni in Bayern Munich.

Instructing Markus Steinhöfer of Salzburg

The Juventus team of 1983/84, winners of Serie A and the Cup Winners' Cup

Passing tactics on to Pin, part of the 1985/86 Serie A-winning team, in the Stadio delle Alpi

A manager who always gets involved, both on and off the pitch

The centre of attention for both fans and the media

Saying goodbye to the Salzburg fans, with Jorge Vargas in background

'What more can I do?'

BENFICA
2004–2005

Giovanni Trapattoni's image suffered somewhat in Italy following the squad's unfortunate Euro campaign. Nevertheless, outside Italy, where his merits as a club coach were given more weight than his disappointments as a national coach, he was still a highly sought after trainer. As such, Trapattoni didn't have to wait too long for a new job offer. Just a few short days after leaving the '*Squadra Azzurra*', Trapattoni was hired to replace Antoinio Camacho – who had moved to Real Madrid – as the new coach of Benfica. The team's management offered Trapattoni the same 300-square-metre house which had formerly been occupied by Camacho. The man from Cusano Milanino, however, refused the offer. After all, why should he move into such a house when he was happy living in a hotel suite? In the evenings, Trapattoni would take strolls through the city centre, enjoying the climate and ambiance which this city on the Atlantic coast had to offer. Once again, Trapattoni was back in his element. He had felt unhappy before. As he once made known during his four-year stint as national trainer, Trapattoni missed the constant teamwork which was required in the leagues. 'I love it each time I stand on the pitch. This is what I was born to do.'

For the second time in his career, Trapattoni decided to take up the challenge of working in a country whose language he did not speak and whose football team was unknown to him. It should therefore be little wonder that he had a hard time getting started in Portugal too. Furthermore, it took some time for the players to adjust to the new trainer's defensive scheme, especially in the beginning.

It had been quite some time since Benfica had been the top club in Portugal. Instead, they saw themselves outstripped by record-breakers FC Porto, who over the last few years had managed to win a total of seven titles, among them the Champions League. Porto was now in another league, both professionally and financially. When Trapattoni arrived, it had been a decade since Benfica had last won a championship. Now, the squad hoped that the Italian coach could revive the team's glorious past, at least partially. Benfica announced the spectacular news of Trapattoni's signing to the club on the day of the Euro 2004 final between Portugal and Greece. Observing how the sports newspapers dealt with Trapattoni's hiring, one got an idea of just how high Benfica's reputation is in Portugal. The coup of having landed the Italian coach received even more headlines than the fact that the national team had missed its shot at a trophy. Apparently,

Benfica was seen as more important even than the 'Selecao'.

The first opportunity which Trapattoni's new club had to challenge the more well-off FC Porto presented itself at the beginning of the season in the Supercup, the pre-season duel between the champions of the Portuguese League and the Cup of Portugal winners. But Benfica couldn't hold their own against Porto. Worse was to come. A few days later, a 0–3 loss in a qualification match in Anderlecht meant that Benfica was eliminated from the Champions League and forced to try its luck in the UEFA Cup.

In Trapattoni's opinion, his team was still no worse than Porto or its local rival, the third-place Sporting Lisbon. Instead, just as he did during his time as trainer at Bayern Munich, the new coach placed his hope in younger players. Above all, Trapattoni went to great lengths to promote the eighteen-year-old midfielder Manuel Fernandes as well as forward João Pereira, who was just twenty. Further, he gave rookies such as goal-keeper Quim Silva and defender Manuel dos Santos Fernandes a chance while simultaneously making use of proven talent such as Nuno Gomez or Simäon Sabrosa. And true to his time as Italy's national trainer, Trapattoni had no problem during his time at Benfica with leaving an international player on the bench if his system required him to do so. Facing VfB Stuttgart at a UEFA Cup match in November, Trapattoni dropped the Slovakian Zlatko Zahovic from the squad because he didn't fit into the coach's counter-attacking approach.

Even though Lisbon lost 0–3, one person from the Portuguese delegation shone that evening in the Gottlieb-Daimler Stadium in Stuttgart: none other than the 'Maestro' himself. Trapattoni even stole the show at the post-match press conference from the victorious Matthias Sammer, Stuttgart's rather reserved coach. Using a pot-pourri of words in Italian, German, Portuguese and English, he explained why the match had been lost, what his team still had to learn, and why Benfica had caved in following a strong first-half per-formance. Once again, he removed a piece of paper from his jacket pocket and began to read from his notes. His return to German that evening had a nostalgic feel to it. In spite of the loss, Benfica managed to survive the group stage, finishing in second place behind Stuttgart, though Trapattoni's squad was later eliminated in the last sixteen by ZSKA Moscow, the eventual UEFA Cup champions.

Support for the team in Lisbon was significant, with several hundred fans appearing at every training practice to show their support for the coach. After two years of constant nagging in Italy about his cautious defensive strategy and his personnel policies, the respect and sym-pathy shown towards him by Benfica fans did Trapattoni good. Even his rudimentary knowledge of Portuguese was not a problem. When he was not on the field, Trapattoni would spend time watching old matches of the Portuguese championship on television. According to Trapattoni, the Portuguese, like the French, focused on speed and were highly influenced by South American and African players. 'They take off at three thousand kilometres per hour and no one can catch up with them,' he once said. Such impressive speed made for an eye-catching spectacle, even if it meant that tactical finesse suffered as a result.

Slowly but surely, Trapattoni began to get the team to play how he wanted them to, and the players started to adjust to his tactics. Though they topped the league early on, Benfica performed poorly over an extended period during the autumn. For almost three months, the team was incapable of winning on the road. Only when it became warmer, in the spring, did they finally come into form. Yet shortly before the end of the season, with the title within their grasp, Trapattoni's team showed signs of nervousness. Nonetheless, in spite of seeing their comfortable advantage as the number one team in their division melt away during the final phase of the season, Trapattoni still managed to guide them to the finish line. Following the 1–1 draw with Boavista Porto on the last day of the season, Benfica were once again crowned champions of the Portuguese Superliga, just three points ahead of their archrivals FC Porto. They achieved this without attaining the lowest number of goals against, as was usual for a Trapattoni-led squad.

The fact that the team was not always capable of fulfilling the Maestro's tactical requirements over the course of the previous nine months was no longer that important: Trapattoni had just won the nineteenth title of his coaching career. That night, 60,000 Benfica fans celebrated into the early hours at the team's stadium, Estadio de Luz in Lisbon, waiting for the chance to welcome the team, which had just won the club's thirty-first national title. To say the least, Trapattoni was impressed. 'I've never seen such fans in my forty years of football,' he said. A few days later, Benfica missed its opportunity of achieving the Double, losing 1–2 against Vitória Setúbal in the Cup of Portugal.

Trapattoni, however, knew that he would be leaving Benfica. He had previously rejected an offer from London to coach Tottenham. Trapattoni always received such offers, but not all of them – such as the one that he received from his wife's hometown of Rome – always came at the right time. He had signed the agreement with Benfica very quickly. One day, Trapattoni had been contacted by the club's management, and the next he was being presented to the fans and the press; sometimes, things move quickly. Nevertheless, the distance from his family proved to be too much for him. Trapattoni wanted to be closer to his son, his daughter and his grandson. In the middle of the season, Trapattoni was talking about feeling homesick. Making public his desire to stay with Benfica and to lead the team to the Champions League, he announced his intention to speak once again with his wife during the championship celebrations. But Paola couldn't be convinced to spend another year in Lisbon. Two days after the missed opportunity of the Cup of Portugal, Trapattoni suddenly ended his stint in Lisbon and returned to Italy.

Little did his wife realise, the return was to be brief.

STUTTGART
2005–2006

The Trapattonis were hardly back in Italy before the German national league came knocking on their door for a third time. At the end of the season, VfB Stuttgart had made the decision to fire Matthias Sammer; the former member of the national squad couldn't quite come to terms with the press, or his surroundings in Swabia. Additionally, Sammer had failed to meet the high expectations people had of him following the successful era of Felix Magath. The fact that the team didn't make it into the Champions League provoked an almost apathetic, depressive mood in a club which just a few years before had made such a splash with its outstanding national and international appearances. Subsequently, Erwin Staudt, the VfB president, was looking for a coach 'with enough charisma to guarantee the future success of the club'. Although Sammer was both meticulous and assertive, he was not up to the mark when it came to teaching and motivating his players. Trapattoni had all of these skills.

His unforgettable, passionate appearance at the press conference following the match between Benfica and Stuttgart in the UEFA Cup had impressed Sammer, who at that point was still Stuttgart's coach. Moreover, the multilingual Italian had good international contacts, which, taking into account the club's intention of rejuvenating the team, was an important factor for Stuttgart's executives when it came to making their decision.

Trapattoni really wanted to take up this offer, yet there was still a problem: he had promised his wife that they would finally live in Milan and that he would pay more attention to his family and grandchildren. Trapattoni thus asked for a bit of time to consider the offer. Paola quickly saw that she was fighting a losing battle, however. 'My wife said: "You love your football more than you do me." She wasn't messing around; she meant it,' he said, admitting that he had promised her a nice holiday on an isolated island as compensation. If she wasn't aware of it already, by the time Trapattoni had a football field built in the backyard of his house, Paola must have known that she would have to share her husband with the biggest passion of his life – until death do them part.

Once he was back in Germany, it was clear that Trapattoni still had a cult status. 'I back again [*sic*],' he said at his presentation. Somehow, Trapattoni had never really said goodbye anyway – at least not with any fanfare. Right after his second stint in Munich, an Italian fashion company signed him up as its 'image promoter' for Germany. For weeks, advertising posters could be seen throughout Munich's city centre which contained a portrait of the 'Maestro'. Later, Trapattoni signed an advertising contract with a Bavarian milk producer, for whom he made a commercial in which he could be seen eating yogurt and talking about German television. Afterwards, in Stuttgart, Trapattoni signed advertising contracts with a mineral-water company and a pastry company. An Italian advertising local Swabian cakes, however, did not exactly provoke a wave of enthusiasm throughout the region.

In the middle of June, Trapattoni signed a two-year contract with Stuttgart. 'I've never experienced someone with so much positive energy, with so much passion,' said Staudt, the Stuttgart president. With only two weeks to go before preparations were to begin for the opening match of the season, there was still a lot of work to do. Andreas Brehme was the first player to be signed. The 1990 World Cup winner had once played for Trapattoni at Inter Milan; now he was to be Trapattoni's assistant. One of the advantages offered by Brehme was the fact that he spoke fluent Italian and could thus serve as an interpreter for Trapattoni during practice sessions. 'I need somebody who understands my work and can explain it to the players,' said Trapattoni. In addition, he received back-up support from a fitness coach and a goalkeeping coach from Italy.

The new team was almost in place, and the majority of major personnel decisions had been made: the German national team's forward, Kevin Kuranyi, had been sold to FC Schalke 04. Likewise, Philipp Lahm had gone back to his former club, Bayern Munich. The brilliant midfielder Aleksander Hleb had also left the club: he had decided to move to Arsenal, and Trapattoni was unable to convince him to stay in Stuttgart. (Or perhaps he didn't want to keep him anyway.) Instead, Stuttgart acquired Daniel Bierofka from Leverkusen, Ludovic Magnin from Bremen, and Thomas Hitzlsperger from Aston Villa. Rumours also began to circulate that Luis Figo, who had recently been let go by Real Madrid, was to strengthen the Stuttgart ranks. In the event, Figo ended up signing with Inter Milan, where the money was better and where he would have the chance of playing in the Champions League.

Having realised that it would be difficult to meet the club's – and the fans' – high expectations with the team he had available, Trapattoni still wanted to sign one or two new players. In fact, VfB had been spoiled by the success of the previous years; the club's aim now was to be one of the best teams in the country while at the same time promoting and expanding the training of younger players. In this sense, Trapattoni was the right man for the job, as he has always been one of the few coaches who has both the heart and the patience for developing new blood.

Thanks to Hleb's transfer, which earned the club a few million euro, money would not be a problem when it came to acquiring new players. But Trapattoni knew, too, that the market had basically dried up already. Stuttgart had wasted too much time on firing Sammer, and the club's management had not acted quickly enough in looking for his replacement.

Almost two thousand fans were present to watch Stuttgart's first training session under Trapattoni. The star of the show was not one of the players but

Trapattoni himself: no one else was asked for as many signatures as the coach. It was hoped that the new trainer, thanks to his charisma, would still be able to sign a well-known player. Before heading off to the training camp, in the Steiermark region, the Maestro spent so much time making telephone calls that he had almost no time to look after the team. But it was worth it: Trapattoni managed to acquire Jon Dahl Tomasson from AC Milan, presenting the Danish forward as Kevin Kuranyi's replacement. A few weeks later, at the beginning of August, Jesper Grönkjaer, Tomasson's fellow player from the Danish national team, was bought from Atletico Madrid to fill the spot left open by Hleb.

Trapattoni was able to get a first impression of his new team in the German League Cup, a tournament of the previous season's five best German national league teams, as well as that year's tournament champion. Following an opening victory against Hertha BSC Berlin, Stuttgart were set to face FC Bayern in the semi-finals. Stuttgart managed to defeat Trapattoni's former club in the new Allianz Arena. Players and coaching staff alike were so happy about the victory that they celebrated as if they had just won the league itself. VfB Stuttgart already considered themselves to be on an equal footing with the mighty team from Munich. A few days later, however, Stuttgart lost 0–1 in the final League Cup match, against Schalke. Their performance did not prove promising for a successful start to the German national league season. Trapattoni criticised the lack of courage and engagement of his players, but then pointed out that the loss had been due to the fact that the club had already suffered several injuries and that preparations had been weak because a number of players had participated in the Confederation Cup over the summer.

Thanks to Trapattoni, there was a good deal of optimism in Stuttgart on the eve of the club's first league match. After all, the rise in the team's professional and commercial value was mostly due to the team's new coach. Luciano Pavarotti, the famous Italian tenor, called Staudt, the team's president, and sent greetings to his 'countryman Giovanni' before inviting the entire management to his farewell concert in Stuttgart in October.

For the locals, Trapattoni might have come from another world. For his part, by coming to Stuttgart, Trapattoni was entering into a new world himself. Although Trapattoni had already experienced what it was like to lead second-ranked teams in Cagliari and Florence, it made a difference whether the clubs were playing in Italy or abroad.

Already during the first match, Trapattoni had demonstrated that he was much more than just a defensive tactician: in spite of being outgunned in the 1–1 game against Duisburg, he let his team remain on the attack, even going so far as to substitute two midfielders with two forwards. It looked as if the Maestro was taking the need for a spectacular offensive strategy seriously – which is exactly what Stuttgart was longing for. Moreover, with the help of the team's marketing department, the new trainer's strategy couldn't just be seen on the field. At the end of Highway 10 in Stuttgart, just before the exit leading to the stadium, a large billboard was hung in which Trapattoni could be seen pointing the way to the match. 'Want fun, turn right' was written on the sign.

But fun is one thing. In the second league match, against Cologne, Trapattoni decided to leave team captain Zvonimir Soldo on the bench, thus bringing insecurity to the entire squad. The thirty-seven-year-old Croatian had only been substituted once in the previous season – for tactical reasons – and following the departure of Kevin Kurayni, Philipp Lahm and Aleksander Hleb, he remained perhaps the only stabilising element in an already fragile squad. Stuttgart lost against Cologne, who were climbing up the league, and the first doubts quickly began to appear as to whether the high expectations for the team could be met. Subsequently, Trapattoni admitted that he hadn't assessed the situation correctly, adding that it would be necessary for him to rethink things. For years, Stuttgart had been accustomed to playing with a 4–4–2 system, with a diamond formation which included a play-maker. Due to the squad's current composition, however, the Italian preferred to use two central-defensive mid-fielders, two attacking wingers, and no playmaker. In real-ity, Trapattoni had planned not to play Soldo at all, but he later realised that the team needed an old hand. And this was not only because of his performance, but above all because of his leadership capabilities in defence.

In the beginning, Trapattoni adopted a system of squad rotation which not everyone understood. He did this 'because we have many players of similar strength', he said, adding that it was necessary to show his team various alternatives. 'What would happen if Soldo left the team or became ill?' In Stuttgart, Trapattoni demonstrated that he had no problem with leaving players with international caps on the bench. The players tried to come to terms with the fact that nobody should be afraid of being kicked off the team. 'It's just part of his philosophy,' said Marcus Babbel, who had already trained with Trapattoni in Munich. The *Frankfurter Allgemeine Zeitung* newspaper once likened Trapattoni to 'a bag of surprises, never predictable and always good for a surprise' – exactly what the Stuttgart fans had experienced with him during his first few weeks in charge.

Trapattoni spoke German from the very beginning, and refused to have an interpreter by his side at all times. But as the misunderstandings grew and he ran the risk of no longer being taken seriously, he finally appeared in public with an interpreter.

But the pressure on Trapattoni continued to grow. He was forced constantly to ask people to be more patient, arguing that he could not put together his team from one day to the next. The last few elements were still missing – as well as the lust for success – but he saw no real difference between his club and a team like Bayern Munich. For quite some time, he had lived by the motto: 'Small situations decide major matches'. Yet it was exactly the fine details which had taken VfB Stuttgart off course every time Trapattoni attempted to show his team the way forward.

Above all, the team lacked the hunger for success. Four matches went by, and Stuttgart still hadn't won a single one. The coach found the players' expectations to be too high. 'The team has enough quality, it just lacks experience,' he commented. The 2–0 victory during the first match of the UEFA Cup tournament against NK Domzale, the first-placed team in the Slovenian league, did little to quell the criticism from both fans and press alike, who felt that it was too little too late, and that in any case the team's performance was anything but impressive. Furthermore, the team's old hands began to complain about their coach in public, probably because some of them had their own ambitions. For his part, club president Staudt began to complain about Trapattoni in public too.

The victory in Mainz, the first of the season, came just at the right time for Trapattoni. But things didn't remain calm for long, and the victory over Mainz was followed a week later by another loss. Stuttgart's first home victory, in their seventh game of the season, as well as the fact that Trapattoni's squad had reached the quarter-finals of the UEFA Cup, wasn't enough to quieten the critics. With fans lacking any sign of an improvement at the club, things began to come to a head. By the end of September, rumours were starting to circulate that the club had begun negotiations to replace Trapattoni with Klaus Augenthaler, Leverkusen's recently released coach. Of course, the team's management denied that such discussions were taking place, yet they didn't completely dispel the rumours either. In the end, Augenthaler signed a contract with Wolfsburg at the end of December.

Stuttgart and Trapattoni were still able to take some cheer from results in the first half of the season. In spite of eleven back-to-back losses, Stuttgart went into the winter break in sixth place, with the chance of participating in Europe still open to them. Moreover, Trapattoni's squad had survived the UEFA Cup's group stage. It seemed as though things were finally about to pick up.

At the winter training camp in Dubai, Trapattoni believed that he had left the most difficult phase of the season behind him. Following several discussions with his players, he decided to change his tactics after having recognised that the constant rotations did more harm than good to the team. 'We have finally understood the trainer's concept,' said Swiss defender Ludovic Magnin. But then things took another turn for the worse: Stuttgart lost their first match of the second half of the season. Worst of all, MSV Duisburg won using the very tactics which were generally associated with Trapattoni: a padlock defence comprised of ten defenders. The temporarily silenced critics re-emerged, but this time louder than ever. And once again, Trapattoni was forced to recognise certain weaknesses. The third consecutive match without a goal – and thus without a victory – in the second half of the season proved to be Trapattoni's last at Stuttgart. Just one day after Stuttgart's 0–0 draw with Bremen, Trapattoni was fired, together with his assistants. This was the first time that this had happened to him in his thirty-three-year career.

'I was angry and couldn't understand why I and my colleagues would be let go from one day to the next. I was convinced that we could get a UEFA Cup spot with this team,' wrote Trapattoni on his website. 'I wanted to keep working with the team. I felt good in Stuttgart: the surroundings were right for me, the players were dedicated to the training, and I had the feeling that, in spite of the disappointment of the first few games of the second half of the season, we were working well together and would enjoy success together. Now we'll never know how it would have ended.'

One of Trapattoni's major problems in Stuttgart had nothing to do with his style, his way of solving problems, or communication difficulties with his players. Rather, he had to find a solution for everything. At Stuttgart, Trapattoni was required to be not only a coach but also an entertainer, and he had to assume responsibilities which were actually the job of the team's manager. He led what was practically a one-man show, at least at the very beginning. And that was something which Trapattoni didn't want. Stuttgart needed someone on the management side who had sufficient knowledge of football so as to be an intermediary between the team and its management. Herbert Briem had taken over the job of manager just one year before Trapattoni was hired, but the fact that he had also to serve as a scout meant that he was overburdened. Even Matthias Sammer, Stuttgart's former coach, had demanded additional support on the footballing side. His request had been denied. It wasn't clear to Trapattoni just what he was getting into. The mistake was finally corrected in the winter break, when former player Horst Heldt took over as manager. But it was too late. Thereafter, Briem played second fiddle to Heldt and could dedicate his time to scouting for new talent.

Furthermore, the executives had failed to realise that Stuttgart's glory days were a thing of the past, and that no wave of a magic wand – even from Trapattoni – could create a successful squad. The Italian probably thought that Stuttgart's management would understand that which was self-evident. Likewise, he could not be expected to realise immediately just how dire the situation was. Trapattoni was confident, right up to the bitter end: 'We belong together,' he said. But he also knew that 'A man and woman may love each other, but they can still separate.'

That the problem did not emanate from the coach became clear only later. At the point when Trapattoni was let go, Stuttgart were sixth in the league, having earned twenty-seven points. Fourteen matches later, at the end of the season, Stuttgart, now led by Armin Veh, finished the season in ninth place, with forty-three points.

After being released from Stuttgart, Trapattoni returned to Italy to take care of his two grandchildren, whom he had seen too little of recently. Thereafter, he watched football on television, and would sometimes go to watch a match at the local stadium. 'It's not particularly exciting, but it does have its appeal. Now I have time to do things which I didn't have time for before,' he wrote on his website. He didn't mention any kind of plans for the future. 'I just let things come as they are,' he said. That was the fifteenth of May. A few days later, he signed a contract with Red Bull Salzburg.

RED BULL SALZBURG
2006–2008

The football season in Austria had been over for five days when Red Bull Salzburg announced a real bombshell on their website. The surprise wasn't that Kurt Jara was being replaced as the runner-ups' trainer, but rather that his successor would be Giovanni Trapattoni. The successful Italian trainer, along with Lothar Matthäus, was given not only the task of making the Salzburg football club the leader of their National League, but of also establishing them as a force on the international stage. Trapattoni was quoted on the club's homepage as saying: 'I am coming to Salzburg, together with Red Bull, to accomplish something big.'

Trapattoni and Austria go together about as well Mozart and hip-hop, so a lot of people thought at first glance that the announcement was just a PR stunt, or a way to keep people talking about Salzburg football throughout the summer break, especially because Trapattoni initially denied the news and announced that a contract had yet to be signed. It seemed like a casual flirtation that didn't show any prospects for a lasting relationship.

The club had acted a little prematurely. The 'Maestro' announced on German television that it would be a couple more weeks until a decision was made. There were still two things that needed to be discussed: his precise job description and how the responsibilities within this well-known trainer's team should be distributed. Trapattoni definitely had a clear agenda. 'I will be the chief trainer and Matthäus will be my assistant.' The owner of the club, Dieter Mateschitz, had the same vision. The points still open for discussion were quickly cleared up and, suddenly, there was nothing standing in the way of a heartfelt connection between Italy and Austria. Four days after the rash announcement on the website, Trapattoni did indeed sign a contract in Salzburg, together with Matthäus, his former playmaker at Bayern. They drank to a future of successful collaboration in Hanger 7 – an aeroplane museum which doubles as a ritzy restaurant – owned by the millionaire Mateschitz.

Giovanni Trapattoni, the world's most successful club coach, had ended up in Austria in a league which not only didn't meet the highest European standards but which also didn't enjoy an especially good international reputation. It was even sometimes ridiculed as the 'Opera League'. Of course, in those days, Trapattoni was often asked why he had decided to take on a new job in Austria, of all places. 'I don't need the big international football names in order to feel good. You can direct anywhere,' he said. 'Those who don't understand why I can work in Austria don't have any idea who Giovanni Trapattoni is.' He was a football enthusiast, kept young by playing the game and by surrounding himself with young players. His wife Paola thought that he should finally start spending more time with his grandchildren, but Trapattoni admits that he couldn't imagine life without football. 'I need the football field, I need the ball.' He also didn't think that the skills level in Austria was as bad as it had been described. In football there is no second class. Austria's task was to refuse to accept their inferior status and 'finally to begin to think in a bigger way, to learn to believe in larger goals'.

And if it was going to be Austria, Red Bull Salzburg was of course the best fit for him. The club represented an entry into a new, successful football world. A year before, the energy-drink maker Dieter Mateschitz had taken over the club and restructured it. At the time, SV Austria Salzburg were facing the possibility of both relegation and financial ruin. Mateschitz had long baulked at the idea of getting into the football business and initially concentrated solely on sponsoring extreme sports. However, there came a time when he didn't want to limit himself any more. As far as marketing was concerned, he declared, there was no more important sport in the world than football. 'It has become an intelligent game of strategy, with football stars who are put on the same level as pop stars. Football has become more socially acceptable than ever before.' Furthermore, the German football icon Franz Beckenbauer, who was acting as an advisor in Salzburg at the time, did a good job of persuading Mateschitz to back the club. In fact, he was also the person who warmly recommended Trapattoni for the post a year later.

Within a couple of months, the millionaire had completely overhauled the club. As well as taking on the name, colours and logo of the energy drink, Salzburg transformed themselves from a relegation candidate into a favourite to win the league. In order to achieve this, Mateschitz sold many of the players: only seven players remained under Kurt Jara from the previous season. The fans were unhappy about this development, and many fought against it: as far as they could see, their previously down-to-earth football club was being transformed into a completely artificial creation.

In the end, Salzburg missed their chance of winning the title by a couple of points, despite having made large investments. That was, however, not the reason for Kurt Jara's dismissal; there were player-transfer inconsistencies in connection with the former national-team player. It was of course clear that Jara had to be replaced by a very well-known coach. As Mateschitz thinks on an international level rather than a national one, Jara's replacement should ideally have been someone who had already won titles and championships and who had secured fame beyond Austria's borders. By hiring Trapattoni, he succeeded in creating a European-wide sensation. The Red Bull owner was himself quite shy with regard to the media; he rarely gave interviews and ran his club like a business in order not to be permanently in the spotlight. He didn't want to be Salzburg's answer to Roman Abramovich: he preferred to make his product the centre of attention and saw everything as a part of a marketing machine designed to boost sales of Red Bull.

However, regardless of the clearly defined skills with-in the coaching team, there were some doubts about whether Lothar Matthäus would accept his role as assistant. The former German international went into coaching soon after the end of his playing career; he started off by making few friends in Austria. Matthäus had his coaching debut with Rapid Vienna and ended up being greatly resented after the team performed worse than ever before in the history of the club, finishing in eighth place. Afterwards, Matthäus quickly switched coaching positions. Although this didn't quite ruin his career, it damaged it significantly. Despite the fact that the position as assistant was a step down, it was still a good opportunity for him. Matthäus didn't only think of Trapattoni in connection with the couple of years they had spent together in Milan and Munich; he treasured the man both as a coach and as a human being, this man whom they also call 'Maestro' in Italy. In addition, he knew how how much Trapattoni loved football. 'Giovanni is a man who needs the pitch,' said Matthäus. Maybe that was why he accepted the secondary role. He did know a couple of the incoming players from his time as a coach in Hungary, Serbia and South America, Matthäus began to play an important role for Trapattoni as early as his first week at Salzburg.

Trapattoni had little time to form a team that was not only ready to dominate the local league but could compete in Europe. The qualifying rounds for the Champions League were held at the end of July, and Trapattoni took it for granted that his team would at least advance to the next level. He generally set high goals for himself in his new job. 'With Salzburg, I would like to get to where I'm used to being – at the highest level.' He therefore fit in perfectly with Mateschitz's vision: to see Red Bull established amongst the fifteen best European football teams within a couple of years.

Speculation about the amount of Red Bull money that would be spent on players ran rampant. Big-name players were suddenly being discussed, stars like Ronaldo, Zé Roberto and Pavel Nedved, who played in renowned clubs and earned very high salaries. Other countries were astonished about what was happening at Salzburg. The newspapers in Italy were regularly reporting events at Salzburg, as were those in Germany and Spain. The team, and Trapattoni, had therefore already fulfilled one of Mateschitz's goals: to carry the name of Red Bull Salzburg around the world.

However, Ronaldo, Zé Roberto and Nedved never signed on for the club, of course. These players' transfer fees and salary expectations were a bit too high, despite the exceptionally high salaries generally paid to footballers in Austria. The trainer-duo knew this. For this reason, Trap-attoni and Matthäus looked first at the German National League and signed Christian Tiffert from VfB Stuttgart, Markus Steinhöfer from Bayern Munich, Niko Kovac from Hertha BSC Berlin, and Timo Ochs and Remo Meyer from TSV 1860 Munich. To complete the squad, they also signed up the leading Swiss player Johan Vonlanthen from PSV Eindhoven, as well as Milan Dudic from Red Star Belgrade, Karel Piták from Slavia Prague, the Chilean Jorge Vargas (who had until recently been playing in Italy), Ramazan Özcan, and Valdimir Janocko from Salzburg's league rivals Rapid Vienna. Eleven new players – the equivalent of an entire team – had to be integrated into the club by the start of the season. In June, preparation began, with seventeen 'foreign legionnaires' from eleven countries, and nearly the same number of Austrians. Two months later, Andreas Ivanschitz left the club. He couldn't see any possibility of getting a permanent place on the team. With his departure, the local contingent lessened to just five players. The fans weren't terribly fond of this trend towards increasing multiculturalism, and the national coach, Josef Hickersberger, worried about whether the Austrian players, and those on the fringes of the squad, could stay the course. Trapattoni not only didn't want to, but also couldn't, take national sensitivities into consideration. He had to play people who would guarantee success, and anyway, 'the young Austrians could learn something from the legionnaires', as he put it.

On the first day of training, Trapattoni held a half-hour talk in Seekirchen am Mondsee. In German. Of course there was a translator at his side, but he enjoyed using his language skills – which he had only just started learning, at the age of almost sixty, and sometimes with the help of a 'cheat sheet'. He ended by giving a lecture on the chances the underdog had against the favourites. 'What is small can always become big. I, too, was no star, and I played against big names like Johan Cruyff.'

The league season began just six weeks later. Red Bull first had to play a couple of matches away from home, as their own ground was being modernised in preparation for the Euro 2008 finals. So Trapattoni had his Austrian-league debut in SV Josko Fenster Ried's Fill-Metallbau Stadium. This was a provincial stadium that held barely eight thousand spectators. Regardless of the famous visitor, the local team asked for an entry fee of just €2. Red Bull had lost there twice in recent years. This time the team won 3–0. Three days later, they travelled to Vorarlberg to play the recently promoted Altach in the Schnabelholz Stadium; a stadium that didn't even meet the already low requirements of the Austrian National League. This trip also ended in success for the Bulls, with a 2–0 win.

It was of course a little unusual for Trapattoni suddenly to be competing in a league in stadiums that he had earlier only seen during friendly matches. It reminded him of when he first started in football. The fans were only an arm's-length away from the coach's bench, but for Trapattoni, who once felt at home in the San Siro and who knows all the biggest football stadiums in Europe, it didn't matter where he worked. The close quarters of the smaller grounds in Ried and Altach didn't bother him. 'A football pitch is a football pitch.' These first two matches were already evidence of the fact that Trapattoni had had an effect on Red Bull's game. In the previous season, a significant weakness when playing away matches had cost the Salzburg team the title. Now, however, with their new impressive defensive strategy, they could convince everyone that they had improved. Trapattoni quickly recognised where Red Bull's weaknesses lay, and before anything else he looked for new defenders. It was probably just a coincidence, and must also have had something to do with Thomas Linke's personality and experience, but the fact that the central defender wore the captain's armband made sense within the new team set-up. This experienced German player took Markus Schopp's position when he left the club. Linke, who had won the UEFA Cup with FC Schalke 04 and who had won the Champions League with Bayern, described how they had started training much more strategically than the year before. However, the new focus on defence, and the fact that they were now playing with only one forward, didn't mean that Salzburg were only forming defensive walls and defending against goals instead of scoring some of their own. That would be demonstrated by their record throughout the season. After the first quarter of the season, Red Bull not only conceded fewer goals than any of their rivals but also scored more than anyone else. However, Ried and Altach didn't exactly belong to the highest rungs in football and were therefore not a good measure of the level of the newly formed Salzburg team.

This was not the case with FC Zürich, their opponents in the second qualifying round for the Champions League. In previous years, Swiss football had gone through a major boom. The national team had made it into the last sixteen the previous summer at the World Cup in Germany. Another Swiss team, FC Basel, had also had two big wins a couple of years before in the Champions League. As a result, Salzburg fans knew that the two matches against Zurich would really test their team. An unexciting performance from Salzburg saw them lose the first leg, in Basel, 1–2, but Trapattoni recognised that there was still a good chance for his team to reach the second and third qualifying rounds; and he was right. Salzburg won the second leg 2–0, with goals from Christian Tiffert and Alexander Zickler, and were thus able to guarantee themselves a place in the UEFA Cup. The Zurich players, Trapattoni said, played '*Patabim, patabim, patabim*': he meant that Salzburg's opponents, although they worked confidently together, weren't particularly effective, unlike his team. Salzburg had played to win – a result that had brought them into the third round against Valencia. 'Football is not like a violin in the theatre, football is about the end result,' Trapattoni explained.

For the first home game of the season, against Grazer AK, Salzburg were also more attack-minded. And in the end, it was more than just wishful thinking. They took the three points, winning 4–1, and went top of the league. Although Red Bull didn't exactly excel themselves in defence, this was perhaps not unexpected, given the tight time schedule and the ongoing integration of new players into the squad. Moreover, the patchy performance was understandable given that the impending contest with Valencia was on all the players' minds. In fact, it was amazing how much in harmony the team was and how confidently they acted during the early season, when they played well enough to take control of the domestic league. However, this didn't necessarily mean that they would be able to stand up to the Spaniards. (Trapattoni was aware of this due to his own painful experience: once, when FC Bayern were favourites to win the first round of the UEFA Cup, they ended up losing against Valencia.) Salzburg's hope was that Valencia wouldn't be in their best shape so early in the season. The championship in Spain began a couple of weeks later than in Austria, and there was artificial grass laid down in the Red Bull arena, which took some getting used to for visiting teams.

Almost everything went according to plan for Salzburg in the home game, thanks to a goal scored by Karel Piták. They were close to getting through to the Champions League proper – much closer than most people would ever have thought. 'Today we made music,' Trapattoni said. The team was definitely not providing the fans with a football opera, but rather with a short symphony concert with a couple of sophisticated passages. Trapattoni got his money's worth with the two matches against Valencia. He fulfilled his long-awaited wish and went to see *Don Giovanni* with his wife Paola. The Trapattonis enjoyed life in Salzburg. Trapattoni had already spent a great of time travelling to Salzburg during the time when he had worked in Munich. They took up residence in an apartment in the centre of the city on the River Salzach, where they were right in the middle of the city's hustle and bustle, which Trapattoni loved. He had also lived close to the central Marienplatz in Munich. All in all, the music-lover Trapattoni (he particularly loves symphonies composed by Bach, Vivaldi, Beethoven and of course Mozart, and has more than three thousand classical-music CDs at home) was in good hands in the home city of the most famous composer in the world.

Then came the second round in Valencia, in the Estadio Luis de Mestalla. The Austrian national team had experienced their worst-ever defeat there: 0–9 against

Spain. In fact, no Austrian club team had ever even secured one point there. Nobody in Red Bull was thinking about that, however. The team were plagued with other worries while travelling to the Iberian peninsula: Alexander Zickler, who had scored seven goals in the six league matches of the season so far, was injured. He had sustained a muscle injury during the league match against SV Mattersburg, which they won 2–0. The German forward, so important to Salzburg due to his defensive abilities, had been given the all-clear and had followed his teammates to Spain. However, after undergoing a fitness test, he ended up on the bench twiddling his thumbs. Salzburg therefore had no chance against the Spanish, who played with three forwards. Even so, the 0–3 defeat was not a fair reflection of Salzburg's performance.

There were no negative consequences for Salzburg in having lost their spot in the Champions League. On the contrary, Salzburg maintained their lead in their league with a 4–0 victory against their competitors, Wacker Innsbruck. They gradually increased their lead at the top, and the public – and the competition – were impressed. But Trapattoni was not yet satisfied. 'One shouldn't assume that everything was already perfect. It's dangerous when you think you're already the champion. We have to be careful not to be overly confident.' Trapattoni was to be proved right when, after nine straight wins, they lost for the first time that season, against Sturm Graz.

Their participation in international competitions was over by September. The English team Blackburn Rovers were too good for Salzburg in the UEFA Cup qualifying round. In the first leg, at home, Salzburg managed a 2–2 draw, but a point was not enough to take to Ewood Park for the return leg two weeks later. In Blackburn, Trapattoni took a great risk and put out three forwards. Unfortunately, the strategy didn't work. The usually strong defence played clumsily, and Red Bull left the European stage with a 0–2 defeat. Trapattoni realised that there there had been a marked deterioration in the team's performance. 'We have to cultivate pride, a will to win, and our own confidence. We still have a lot to learn.'

Trapattoni and his team continued to grow together, regardless of their failure to play in the Champions League and the fact that they were out after the first round of the UEFA Cup. The Italian knew some of the players from before, including Alexander Zickler and Christian Tiffert. As for the others, he quickly got an idea of what they were like. Even at the age of sixty-seven, he still personally demonstrated every exercise during practice.

After winning the title the previous season, Trapattoni was not able to repeat the feat in 2007/08. After thirty-six games, Rapid Vienna were on sixty-nine points, with Red Bull the runners-up, on sixty-three. It is clear that Salzburg lost the battle for the title in their away matches. In eighteen games, they won only three matches, with eight draws and seven defeats. (Rapid had eight wins, four draws and six defeats in their away fixtures.) At home, playing on artifical grass, Salzburg were the best team, with fifteen wins, one draw and two defeats, against Rapid's thirteen wins, two draws and three defeats.

Interestingly, Salzburg lost the most important match

for the title against Rapid at home, on 23 March 2008. This was a historical moment for both Red Bull Salzburg (it was their biggest defeat since the club was re-founded, in 2005) and Trapattoni (for whom it was the biggest defeat of his career). Salzburg were two points ahead going into the match. If they had won, the title would have been in Trapattoni's hands again. But Salzburg lost 7–0.

Trapattoni said: 'This wasn't a defeat. This was a catastrophe. In forty years of my professional career, I never ever got seven goals against. Not as a player, not as a coach.' Fans wrote in various Internet forums about the 'debacle of the century'. Salzburg had played like a second-division team, and nobody could believe what they had seen. Peter Pacult, coach of Rapid Vienna, said weeks later: 'You see the first shot, and it's a goal. Then you see the second shot, and it's another goal, and so on. And at a certain point, you don't believe what you are seeing any more. A game like this happens only every hundred years.'

The twenty-third of March 2008 was the sad conclusion of a season which hadn't started very well for Red Bull. In the Champions League qualifying round, Salzburg won the first leg at home against Schachtjor Donezk 1–0. In the away leg, they went 1–0 up early on thanks to a goal from Remo Meyer, but Donezks Lucarelli then equalised for Donezk, and in the second half the Austrians were firmly on the back foot. In the seventy-eighth minute, Castiollo scored with a penalty, making it 2–1 to Donezk, and just three minutes before the end the Brazilian Brandao got a third goal – and ended Salzburg's chances of making it through to the Champions League group stage. 'Donezk were the better team,' the Maestro said, 'but the penalty wasn't correct. If you award a penalty for that type of physical contact, you have to give ten in a match. We have to focus on the UEFA Cup now.'

But Salzburg did equally poorly in that competition. Salzburg lost in Athens against AEK 0–3 and won at home only 1–0. The national cup competition was not played because of Euro 2008, hosted by Austria and Switzerland, and to give the national team some extra times for preparation. As we have seen, their chances of winning the league disappeared on 23 March.

Football has changed over the years, and so have the players, but Giovanni Trapattoni maintains the leadership style that has been so successful for him in Italy in the past. 'I'm like a father. You have to help the young ones; they can talk to me about anything.' He was also sometimes a strict father in Salzburg, scolding his children when they once again hadn't done as they were told. However, most of the time he just had a lot of fun.

The Republic of Ireland National Team 2008–

It took the FAI one hundred and thirteen days to appoint Giovanni Trapattoni as manager of the Irish football team, and almost a hundred of those days passed before the Italian emerged as a potential successor to Stephen Staunton.

The protracted and bewildering quest for the new gaffer was determined by the intriguing manner of Staunton's departure, announced by FAI chief executive John Delaney in a hotel near Dublin Airport in the early hours of 24 October 2007.

Ireland's most-capped player had been a dead man walking for the seven days since his team narrowly avoided a home defeat to Cyprus in a Euro 2008 qualifier. Steve Finnan's equaliser in the dying seconds of injury time prevented the worst home result in Ireland's football history, but it wasn't enough to silence those calling for the heads of both Staunton and Delaney.

Staunton shows no sign of walking voluntarily, despite the whimpering Irish performance – which had been preceded by talk of revenge for a 5–2 beating away to Cyprus earlier in the dismal campaign. Two years into a four-year contract, the Louthman is determined to see the job through.

But even the less astute observers of FAI politics can see the writing on the wall when, in the fallout from the draw with Cyprus, Delaney distances himself from the appointment of Staunton.

The move sharpens criticism of the chief executive. He led the three-man committee which selected the rookie manager in January 2006, after first promising to replace Brian Kerr with a 'world-class' manager.

Announcing Staunton's departure by 'mutual consent', Delaney re-manoeuvres. In almost the one breath, Delaney both accepts 'the majority of the responsibility for my part in the appointment' of Staunton and declares that he will not be involved in the search for the new manager.

Says Delaney: 'I will not have a direct role in relation to the appointment. We will let football professionals go and deal with the appointment of our next manager.' Not for the first time, the Waterford native earns comparisons with the dark prince Machiavelli.

More significantly, Delaney establishes the fundamental characteristic of the recruitment drive. There will be no swift action, no quick fix. Before the FAI can appoint their king, they must appoint their kingmakers.

And long before the kingmakers are appointed, former England manager Terry Venables is favoured to be the new king. RTÉ football panellist Eamon Dunphy launches a barbed attack on Venables, who later claims that the criticism cost him the job. While this is highly contentious, Dunphy's salvo signals the second fundamental dimension to the recruitment process: the influence of RTÉ's highly popular panel of football experts.

First, Dunphy's sometime RTÉ colleague Graeme Souness declares his interest in the position. Then, more dramatically, John Giles approaches former Wigan manager Paul Jewell about the job. Jewell rules himself out, and in doing so reveals that John Delaney directly asked him to reconsider. Delaney claims that this was no more than a courtesy call, yet the situation highlights his practical difficulty in being completely removed from the recruitment process.

Despite the array of names linked with the job, Venables becomes the firm front-runner when he is sacked as England assistant manager, along with boss Steve McClaren, after the side's failure to reach Euro 2008.

In late November, Republic of Ireland Under-21 boss Don Givens and former England coach Don Howe are confirmed as the FAI's kingmakers. Former Ireland midfielder and (inevitably) RTÉ panellist Ray Houghton becomes the third kingmaker in early December. The headhunters are tasked with interviewing between twelve and fifteen interested candidates.

Meanwhile, the FAI suffers badly from comparisons with the counterparts across the water. Not only does the English FA announce the sacking of McClaren in daylight hours, they also take considerably less time in appointing Fabio Capello as their new manager than the FAI does in appointing its kingmakers.

Christmas and the beginning of the New Year pass without visible progress, and the circle of names linked with the job widens. There seems to be a creeping inevitability about Venables' appointment, as the FAI comes under increasing pressure to make an appointment. Ireland's final qualifying-campaign fixture, away to Wales, the World Cup draw in South Africa, and the World Cup fixture negotiations in Sofia all come and go without Ireland having a permanent figurehead in place.

Although Delaney insists that there is no deadline to be met, two key dates are pressing: the FAI board meeting of 22 January, and the home friendly fixture against Brazil on 6 February.

Prompted by suggestions that a lack of money is holding up progress, the chief executive insists that the FAI is not ruling out paying compensation to secure the services of the headhunters' preferred man. What Delaney does not reveal is that telecoms multimillionaire Denis O'Brien contacted the association two days after the draw with Cyprus – before Staunton had been removed from his post – about providing support in expectation of a change in manager. The FAI now has the financial backing to make the highest-profile appointment in its history.

Although Don Givens claims that progress is being made, there is no announcement about the vacant position at the FAI board meeting in late January. The same day, Steve Finnan announces his retirement from international football, joining both Stephen Carr and Andy O'Brien in retirement post-Staunton. Richard Dunne suggests that the endless wait for a new manager may send other frustrated senior players over the edge.

With Delaney confirming that an appointment is 'very close', each day brings a betting surge strongly favouring a new champion.

On Tuesday 29 January, one Irish bookmaker places Red Bull Salzburg manager Giovanni Trapattoni at odds of 150/1.

The following day, Trapattoni is 7/4.

The sixty-eight-year-old is a seven-times Serie A winner and former coach of the Italian national team; his sudden flash across the radar seems too good to be true. The speculation is dismissed by all concerned. 'I admire the imagination of certain people,' comments Trapattoni. 'Two weeks ago, I was being linked with Africa. Last week, it was England, and now we are talking to Ireland. I'm curious to see where I will be next week.' Red Bull Salzburg also state that no approach has been made.

The FAI declares itself unaware of any link, while Don Givens says: 'When I see that story, I find it absolutely amazing, because we haven't spoken to Trapattoni, and I find it rather hard to believe that the FAI are going behind our backs.'

But the Italian has indeed emerged from nowhere as the preferred candidate. The FAI, and most probably Delaney, were made aware of Trapattoni's interest and alerted Givens, who later said that he couldn't recall exactly who suggested the Italian. The kingmakers ran with it, and frantic behind-the-scenes manoeuvrings began. A spell with Swiss club Neuchâtel Xamax in his playing days proves vital for Givens, who contacts the former club president and associate of Trapattoni, Gilbert Facchinetti. Through Facchinetti, Givens speaks directly with Trapattoni and establishes preliminary discussions over the Ireland job. 'His interest in the job was immediately very positive,' said Givens.

Trapattoni then phones one of his former charges (and RTÉ football panellist) Liam Brady. The Arsenal youth director, who won two Serie A titles under Trapattoni at Juventus, gives his former coach a positive report of the squad, the FAI and the Irish fans.

'I subsequently spoke to Mr Trapattoni three or four times on the phone and it got more positive each time,' said Givens.

There are hopes of an announcement in time for the FAI International Awards in City West the following Sunday, but with Givens preparing the Irish team for the Brazil friendly, and Trapattoni preoccupied with club commitments, a meeting with the headhunters proves impossible to arrange.

Givens confirms over the weekend that one person has yet to be interviewed, while an FAI statement says that an appointment will be made in the next ten days. In public at least, it remains a two-horse race. Shortly after being named International Senior Player of the Year, Richard Dunne names Terry Venables as his preferred choice of manager. A sense of finality is overwhelming, with Brian Kerr imploring: 'For God's sake appoint someone, and let's get the show back on the road quickly.'

Venables uses the following weekend's newspapers to declare that he is still in the running for the job. But in reality, the decision has already been made.

'We went to Salzburg on Sunday – Ray Houghton, Don Howe and myself,' said Don Givens. 'We were picked up from the hotel where we were staying by Mr Trapattoni. He took us to his home, where we had a two-hour meeting with him. It was a very enjoyable meeting for us: to be talking football with that man was exceptional for us. After that, we came back to the hotel. We had a half-an-hour-long meeting amongst ourselves, and at that time we knew that was our man.'

The English sports agent Jerome Anderson, head of the highly influential Sports Media and Entertainment group, acts as intermediary between the parties. John Delaney travels to Trapattoni's representatives in Milan for the conclusion of the talks.

Contracts are signed on Tuesday 12 February, enabling the FAI to announce on the eve of Valentine's Day that they have their man.

Hours before the Abbotstown press conference begins, Trapattoni confirms his new position from Salzburg.

'This is the time in a year when football managers receive offers, and this is what has happened to me,' says Trapattoni. 'In the last two weeks, I received offers from various clubs, and about ten days ago representatives of the Football Association of Ireland approached me. I found their offer very interesting.

'I am very comfortable here in Salzburg. We won the Austrian title last year and we have a great chance to win the title again this year. Leaving the title as a farewell present to my Bulls is now my number-one aim.

'But the opportunity to manage the Irish team will give me a lot more time to spend with my family. Yesterday my lawyers in Milan and representatives of the FAI came to an agreement, and I accepted their offer.'

Liam Brady is also expected to have a role in the new management set-up. 'I know Liam from our mutual time at Juventus,' says Trapattoni. 'I called him and asked him for his thoughts on my commitment with the FAI, and when he said it was OK, I asked him for assistance if needed.'

Trapattoni's commitments with Red Bull Salzburg keep him preoccupied until May, but he speaks enthusiastically of qualifying for the World Cup finals in South Africa with Ireland in a group that also includes Italy.

'Ireland are not a second-rate team; they are supposed to be a first-rate team. Qualifying for the World Cup in 2010 will be hard, and playing against the Italian team will make me proud, but it should be possible for Ireland to come first.'

In Abbotstown, there is a sense of satisfaction at the masterstroke that has secured a manager of the highest calibre. 'There were certain boxes to be ticked, and Trapattoni ticked all of them,' beams Givens. 'Regardless of the time factor, we certainly have a feeling now that all's well that ends well. We got the top man, albeit it took longer than we'd hoped.'

John Delaney reveals that Trapattoni has been given a two-year contract, which can be extended if both parties are satisfied. He goes some way to clarifying the role of Jerome Anderson, saying that the agent made an important contribution to finalising the contract discussions.

Delaney also confirms that half the salaries of Trapattoni and his back-room staff are to be paid for by Denis O'Brien, saying that O'Brien's offer was a 'pivotal moment' in the recruitment process. 'There has been no pressure, either internally or externally, on the three-man subcommittee to make a particular appointment,' he stresses.

O'Brien commends the FAI. 'I think there's maybe ten people involved in this. I think all the credit should go to John Delaney and the committee, and I think the FAI. The criticism they have received over the last three months was very, very hard but they stuck to their guns and now they've the right man.'

Former Italy international midfielder Marco Tardelli is confirmed as Trapattoni's assistant, with Fausto Rossi joining as fitness coach. Tardelli himself has experience of the hot seat, having managed the Italian Under-21s, Inter Milan and the Egyptian national team.

In March, Liam Brady agrees a two-year deal to assist the new Republic of Ireland manager, and will combine the role with his position at Arsenal's youth academy. 'I was a senior international player for sixteen years, from when I was eighteen until I was thirty-four, and I am really looking forward to working with Giovanni Trapattoni and trying to qualify for the World Cup Finals,' he says.

'I've worked first-hand with the man. He had a great knowledge of the game, he was great tactically, and I just think he ticks all the boxes. He's also a great person. I'm not exaggerating when I say I really think these players will enjoy playing under him.'

Trapattoni is officially unveiled as Ireland boss on 1 May. He expresses hopes of talking Finnan and O'Brien out of retirement, as well as bringing the exiled Stephen Ireland in from the cold. 'We will talk to those players who have retired from international football, but who are still playing at a high level,' he says. 'They have to decide over the next few weeks if they want to be involved. Stephen Ireland is a very important player for us. He is young but he has quality.'

It's hard to see any player saying 'no' to the man. Although speaking with limited English, Trapattoni has no problem in communicating his passion for the game or getting his message across.

'I am looking forward to the challenge. It will be difficult, as we are in a tough group with five other very good teams, but I trust my team. We are all friends and we will work together,' says Trapattoni of his back-room team, which now includes former internationals Frank Stapleton, Mick Martin and Alan Kelly.

'I have always sought a challenge to bring out the best in me. When Don Givens called me and asked me if I would be interested in becoming Ireland manager, I became very excited. At that moment, I was working in Salzburg, but I needed a new experience, and I think this job is the right one at the right time for me.'

Confessing that he sometimes acts on impulse, Trapattoni says that he was contacted by other national teams and clubs in Italy, but was immediately enthusiastic about the Ireland job once Brady assured him that it was a good opportunity.

Although some of Ireland's leading lights have dimmed in recent times, with Damien Duff struggling to regain his past form and Shay Givens's career now dogged by injury, Trapattoni is upbeat: 'I came here because we have good players and every possibility of qualifying. We have players who have experience. With good players and good organisation, we have good possibilities.'

Despite the euphoria of the Trapattoni coup, the Irish team are at their lowest ebb in more than twenty years. The sporting public awaits with interest the character of Trapattoni's Ireland. He was reared at AC Milan on the defensive, *catenaccio* style and has favoured safety-first tactics ever since. The only blot on an otherwise peerless CV was with Italy between 2000 and 2004. Italy exited the 2002 World Cup after a shock defeat by hosts South Korea, and his cautious tactics at Euro 2004 also led to an early departure. His defensive style may come as a surprise to fans envisaging Trapattoni as a cure for all of Ireland's ills. But as he points out: 'A beautiful game is for twenty-four hours in the newspapers; a result stands forever.'

Whatever style evolves, there will be no Trapattoni revolution. 'It's very dangerous to change a lot in one game or two games. You must change little situations. I cannot change their habits immediately. I have worked before with players of many cultures, and it is important that they work together. If I didn't have trust in the challenge ahead, I would not be here.'

Trapattoni, like all Irish managers before him, must get the national side punching above its weight. To do so, the team must be well organised and motivated, qualities that have been lacking under recent regimes. There is little to suggest that Trapattoni will falter.

One thing is clear about Giovanni Trapattoni, the man who in 1998 famously said '*Ich habe fertig*' ('I have through'): he hasn't finished yet. The wait is over. Let the journey begin.

STATISTICS

BIOGRAPHICAL INFORMATION

Born on 17 March 1939 on Via 24 maggio in Cusano Milanino

Father Francesco, mother Romilda, siblings Maria, Elisabetta, Antonio, Angela (all older than Giovanni)

1964, married to Paola Miceli, whom he met during the Olympic Games in Rome in 1960; one daughter, Alessandra, one son, Alberto; two grandchildren

TRAPATTONI'S CAREER AS A PLAYER

CLUBS

1959/60, MILAN

Two games; third place in the Championship, out in the second round of the Cup, 0–1 against Como

1960/61, MILAN

Thirty games, one goal (16 April 1961, against Roma), one own goal (2 April 1961, against Napoli); second place in the league, out of the Cup in the last sixteen, 1–2 against Goalino

1961/62, MILAN

Thirty-two games; league winner; out of the Cup in the second round, 0–1 against Modena. Eliminated in the first round of the Inter Cities Fairs Cup against Novi Sad XI (0–0, 0–2).

1962/63, MILAN

Thirty games; third place in the league, out of the Cup in the last sixteen, 0–1 against Sampdoria. European Cup winner, 2–1 against Benfica Lisbon on 22 May 1963 in London. World Club Championship: lost to Santos (4–2, 2–4, 0–1; Trapattoni scored a goal in first game).

1963/64, MILAN

Twenty-eight games, one goal (on 12 January 1964 against Spal); third place in the league; out of the Cup in the last sixteen, 0–1 against Fiorentina. Eliminated in the last sixteen in the European Cup against Real Madrid (1–4, 2–0).

1964/65, MILAN

Thirty games; second place in the league; out of the Cup in the first round, 1–2 against Simmenthal Monza. Eliminated in the first round of the Inter Cities Fairs Cup against Strasbourg (0–2, 0–1).

1965/66, MILAN

Eighteen games, one goal (22 May 1966 against Catania); seventh place in the league, out of the Cup in the quarter-finals 1–3 against Fiorentina. Eliminated in the last sixteen of the Inter Cities Fairs Cup against Chelsea (2–1, 1–2, 1–1, Chelsea won on drawing of lots). Note: in the first round against Strasbourg, and in the second round against CUF Barreiro, Milan needed three games to progress (and also won the draw against Strasbourg). All three deciding games were in Milan.

1966/67, MILAN

Twenty-three games; eighth place in the league; Cup winner on 14 June 1967, 1–0 against Padova

1967/68, MILAN

Twenty-four games; Championship winner; second in Cup competition in the final four group. International: winner of the Cup

Winners' Cup on 23 May 1968 in Rotterdam, 2–0 against Hamburg
SV.

1968/69, MILAN

Twenty-two games; second place in the Championship (level on
points with Cagliari); out of the Cup in quarter-finals, 0–1 against
Goalino. International: winner of the National Cup on 28 May
1969 in Madrid, 4–1 against Ajax Amsterdam. World Club Cup
winner, 3–0, 1–2 against Estudiantes.

1969/70, MILAN

Twenty games, one own goal (12 April 1970 against Fiorentina 2–3,
final score 2–4); fourth place in the Championship, out of the Cup
in the first group stage due to finishing in second place, behind
Varese. International: out in second round of the National Cup
against Feijenoord (1–0, 0–2), who were coached by Ernst Happel.

1970/71, MILAN

Fifteen games; second place in the Championship, second in Cup
competition in the final four group.

1971/72, VARESE

Ten games; sixteenth place in the Championship (facing relegation); out of the Cup in the first group stage due to finishing in second place behind Inter Milan.

SQUAD DETAILS OF LEAGUE-WINNING TEAMS

1961/62

Ghezzi (27 games), Liberalato (7), David (30), Salvadore (30),
Zagatti (8), Trebbi (5), Trapattoni (32), Maldini (34), Radice (28),
Pelagalli (14), Danova (17), Sani (20), Altafini (33), Rivera (27),
Barison (22), Pivatelli (16), Greaves (10), Conti (9), Ghiggia (4),
Lodetti (1).

Technical director: Giuseppe Viani. Coach: Nereo Rocco.

1967/68

Cudicini (18), Belli (12), Vecchi (1), Anquiletti (30), Schnellinger
(27), Baveni (4); Rosato (28), Malatrasi (28), Trapattoni (24), Scala

(7); Hamrin (23), Lodetti (29), Sormani (29), Rivera (29), Prati (23), Mora (9), Golin (4), Angelillo (3), Rognoni (2), Giacomini (1).

Coach: Nereo Rocco.

FINALS OF EUROPEAN MATCHES

EUROPEAN CUP, 1962/63

Wembley Stadium, London, 22 May 1963

Spectators: 45,000

Referee: Arthur Holland (England)

AC Milan–Benfica Lisbon: 2–1 (0–1).

Goals: 0–1 Eusébio (19'), 1–1 Altafini (58'), 2–1 Altafini (70')

AC Milan: Ghezzi; David, Maldini, Trebbi; Benitez, Trapattoni, Pivatelli, Sani, Altafini, Rivera, Mora.

SL Benfica: Costa Pereira, Cavem, Cruz, Humberto, Raul, Coluna, Santana, Augusto, Goalres, Eusébio, Simoes.

WORLD CLUB CHAMPIONSHIP, 1963

FIRST LEG

San Siro Stadium, Milan, 16 October 1963

Spectators: 60,500

AC Milan–Santos: 4–2 (2–0)

Goals: 1–0 Trapattoni (3'), 2–0 Amarildo (15'), 2–1 Pelé (55'), 3–1 Amarildo (67'), 4–1 Mora (82'), 4–2 Pelé (84', penalty)

AC Milan: Ghezzi, David, Trebbi, Pelagalli, Maldini, Trapattoni, Mora, Lodetti, J. Altafini, Rivera, Amarildo.

Santos: Gilmar, Lima, Haroldo, Calvet, Geraldinho, Mengalvio, Zito, Dorval, Coutinho, Pelé, Pepe.

SECOND LEG

Maracaná, Rio de Janeiro, 14 November 1963

Spectators: 150,000

Referee: Juan Regis Brozzi (Argentina)

Santos–AC Milan: 4–2 (0–2)

Goals: 0–1 Altafini (12'), 0–2 Mora (17'), 1–2 Pepe (50'), 2–2 Almir or Mengalvio (54'), 3–2 Lima (65'), 4–2 Pepe (68').

Santos: Gilmar, Ismael, Mauro, Haroldo, Dalmo, Lima, Mengalvio, Dorval, Coutinho, Almir, Pepe.

AC Milan: Ghezzi, David, Trebbi, Pelegalli, Maldini, Trapattoni, Mora, Lodetti, J. Altafini, J. Rivera, Amarildo.

DECIDING GAME

Maracaná, Rio de Janeiro, 16 November 1963

Spectators: 150,000

Referee: Juan Regis Brozzi (Argentina)

Santos–AC Milan: 1–0 (1–0)

Goal: Dalmo (31', penalty)

Santos: Gilmar; Ismael (red), Mauro, Haroldo, Dalmo, Lima, Mengalvio, Dorval, Coutinho, Almir, Pepe.

AC Milan: Balzarini (Barluzzi), Benítez, Pelegalli, Trebbi, Maldini (red), Trapattoni, Mora, Lodetti, Altafini, Mazzola, Amarildo, Fortunato.

CUP WINNERS' CUP, 1967/68

Feyenoord Stadium, Rotterdam, 23 May 1968

Spectators: 53,000

Referee: José Ortiz de Mendíbil (Spain)

AC Milan–Hamburg SV: 2–0 (2–0)

Goals: 1–0 Hamrin (3'), 2–0 Hamrin (19')

AC Milan: Cudicini, Anquilletti, Schnellinger, Rosato, Scala, Trapattoni, Lodetti, Hamrin, Sormani, Rivera, Prati

Hamburg SV: Ozcan, Sandmann, Schulz, Horst, Kurbjuhn, Dieckmann, Kramer, B.Dörfel, Seeler, Honig, G. Dörfel

EUROPEAN CUP, 1968/69

Bernabeu Stadium, Madrid, 28 May 1969

Spectators: 31,000

AC Milan–Ajax Amsterdam: 4–1 (2–0)

Goals: 1–0 Prati (7'), 2–0 Prati (40'), 2 –1 Vasovic (60', penalty), 3–1 Sormani (67'), 4–1 Prati (75')

AC Milan: Cudicini, Malatrasi, Anquilletti, Schnellinger, Rosato, Trapattoni, Lodetti, Rivera; Hamrin, Sormani, Prati

Ajax: Bals, Suurbier (Muller), Hulshoff, Vasovic, Van Duivenbode, Pronk, Groot (Nuninga), Swart, Cruijff, Danielsson, Keizer

WORLD CLUB CHAMPIONSHIP, 1969

FIRST LEG

San Siro, Milan, 8 October 1969

Spectators: 60,500

Referee: Roger Machin (France)

AC Milan–Estudiantes de La Plata: 3–0 (2–0)

Goals: Sormani (2), Combin (1).

AC Milan: Cudicini, Malatrasi, Anquiletti, Rosato, Schnellinger, Lodetti, Rivera, Fogli, Sormani, Combin (Rognoni), Prati.

Estudiantes LP: Poletti, Aguirre-Suárez, Medina, Madero, Malbernat, Bilardo, Togneri, Echecopar (Ribaudo), Flores, Conigliaro, Verón.

SECOND LEG

La Bombonera, Buenos Aires, 22 October 1969

Spectators: 45,000

Referee: Domingo Massalo Conley (Chile)

Estudiantes de La Plata–Milan: 2–1 (2–1)

Goals: Aguirre-Suárez, Conigliaro/Rivera.

Estudiantes LP: Poletti, Manera, Aguirre-Suárez, Madero, Malbernat, Bilardo (Echecopar), Romero, Togneri, Conigliaro, Taverna, Verón.

Milan: Cudicini, Malatrasi (Maldera), Anquiletti, Fogli, Rosato, Schnellinger, Lodetti, Rivera, Sormani, Combin, Prati (Rognoni).

APPEARANCES FOR THE NATIONAL TEAM

Matches played: 17 (12 wins, 2 draws, 3 losses, goal difference 38–7)

Goals: 1 (9 June 1963 against Austria, 1–0, final score 1–0)

First match: 10.12.1960 against Austria, 12

First match: 05.12.1964 against Denmark, 3–1

	DATE	PLACE	OPPONENT	RESULT
1	10.12.60	Naples	Austria	1–2
2	25.04.61	Bologna	Northern Ireland	3–2
3	24.05.61	Rome	England	2–3
4	15.06.61	Florence	Argentina	4–1
5	15.10.61	Tel Aviv	Israel	4–2
6	04.11.61	Turin	Israel	6–0
7	13.05.62	Brussels	Belgium	3–1
8	11.11.62	Vienna	Austria	2–1
9	27.03.63	Istanbul	Turkey	1–0
10	12.05.63	Milan	Brazil	3–0
11	09.06.63	Vienna	Austria	1–0
12	13.10.63	Moscow	USSR	0–2
13	10.11.63	Rome	USSR	1–1
14	14.12.63	Turin	Austria	1–0
15	11.04.64	Florence	CSSR	0–0
16	10.05.64	Lausanne	Switzerland	3–1
17	05.12.64	Bologna	Denmark	3–1

1960 OLYMPIC FOOTBALL TOURNAMENT IN ROME

PRELIMINARY ROUND
26 August 1960, Stadio Fuorigrotta, Naples
4–1 against Taiwan

29 August 1960, Stadio Flaminio, Rome
2–2 against Great Britain

1 September 1960, Stadio Municipal, Florence
3–1 against Brazil

SEMI-FINAL

5 September 1960, Stadio Fuorigrotta, Naples
1–1 against Yugoslavia (Italy lost after lots were drawn)

THIRD-PLACE PLAY-OFF

9 September 1960, Stadio Flaminio, Rome
1–2 against Hungary

TRAPATTONI'S COACHING CAREER

AT CLUB LEVEL

1972/73, MILAN (UNDER-21 TEAM)
One game, 3–5 against Verona, when Trapattoni replaced the suspended Nereo Rocco

1973/74, MILAN (UNDER-21 TEAM)
Six games, when Giovanni Trapattoni replaced Cesare Maldini, who had been fired

1974/75, MILAN (FIRST TEAM)
League, fifth place; Cup, second, lost on 28 June 1975 in Rome 2–3 against Fiorentina

1975/76, MILAN
League, third place; out of the Cup in the quarter-finals. Eliminated in the quarter-finals of the UEFA Cup, 0–2, 2–1 against Club Brugge, coached by Ernst Happel.

1976/77, JUVENTUS
League winners; out of the Cup in the quarter-finals. UEFA Cup winner against Athletico Bilbao, 1–0, 1–2. It was the first European title for Juventus.

1977/78, JUVENTUS

League winners; out of the Cup in the quarter-finals. Lost in the European Cup semi-finals, 1–0, 0–2 after extra time against Club Brugge, coached by Ernst Happel.

1978/79, JUVENTUS

League, third place; Cup winners, won on 20 June 1979 in Naples 2–1 after extra time against Palermo. Eliminated in the first round of the European Cup, 1–0, 0–2 against Glasgow Rangers.

1979/80, JUVENTUS

League, second place; out of the Cup in the semi-finals against Goalino. Lost in the Cup Winners' Cup semi-finals, 1–1, 0–1 against Arsenal.

1980/81, JUVENTUS

League winner; out of the Cup in the semi-finals against Rome. Eliminated in the UEFA Cup second round, 3–1, 1–3, 1–4 PSO against Widzew Lódz.

1981/82, JUVENTUS

League winner; out of the Cup in the qualifying round. Eliminated in the second round of the European Cup, 1–3, 1–1 against Anderlecht.

1982/83, JUVENTUS

League, second place, Cup winner, 0–2, 3–0 after extra time against Hellas Verona. Runners-up in European Cup, losing 0–1 on 25 May 1983 in Athens against Hamburg SV, coached by Ernst Happel. In the same year, Juventus won the 'Mundialito de Clubs', a top-class summer tournament in Milan.

1983/84, JUVENTUS

League winner; out of the Cup in the last sixteen, 1–2, 2–2 against Bari. Winner of the Cup Winners' Cup, 2–1 on 16 May 1984 against FC Porto in Basel. Winner of the UEFA Super Cup, 2–0 in Turin against Liverpool FC.

1984/85, JUVENTUS

League, sixth place; out of the Cup in the quarter-finals, 0–0, 0–1 against Milan. Winners of the European Cup, 1–0 in Brussels against Liverpool FC. Due to the English team's disqualification, the UEFA Super Cup did not take place (Everton won the Cup Winners' Cup). World Club Cup winners, 4–2 in penalty shoot-out in Tokyo against Boca Juniors of Argentina.

1985/86, JUVENTUS
League winner; out of the Cup in the last sixteen, 0–1, 1–1 against Como. Eliminated in the quarter-finals of the European Cup, 0–1, 1–1 against Barcelona.

1986/87, INTER
League, third place; out of the Cup in the quarter-finals, 1–1, 4–6 PSO against Cremonese. Eliminated in the UEFA Cup quarter-finals, 0–0, 1–1 against Göteborg.

1987/88, INTER
League, fifth place; out of the Cup in the semi-finals, 0–0, 0–1 against Sampdoria Genua. Eliminated in the third round of the UEFA Cup, 1–1, 0–1 against Espanol

1988/89, INTER
League winner; out of the Cup in the second group stage. Winner of the Italian Super Cup, 2–1 against Sampdoria. Eliminated in the third round of the UEFA Cup, 2–0, 1–3 against Bayern Munich. (The 1–3 defeat was Trapattoni's hundredth game on the European stage.)

1989/90, INTER
League, third place; out of the Cup in the quarter-finals. Eliminated in the first round of the European Cup, 0–1, 1–1 against Malmö FF.

1990/91, INTER
League, third place; out of the Cup in the last sixteen, 2–1, 0–1 against Torino. Winners of the UEFA Cup, 2–0, 0–1 against Roma.

1991/92, JUVENTUS
League runners-up; runners-up in the Cup, 1–0, 0–2 against Parma.

1992/93, JUVENTUS
League, fourth place; out of the Cup in the semi-finals, 1–1, 2–2

against Goalino. Winners of the UEFA Cup, 3–1, 3–0 against Borussia Dortmund.

1993/94, JUVENTUS

League, second place; out of the Cup in the second round, 1–1, 3–4 against Venezia. Eliminated in the quarter-finals of the UEFA Cup, 0–1, 1–2 against Cagliari.

1994/95, BAYERN MUNICH

Bundesliga, fifth place; out of the Cup in the first round, 0–1 against TSV Vestenbergsgreuth. Eliminated in the semi-finals of the Champions League, 0–0, 2–5 against Ajax Amsterdam.

1995/96, CAGLIARI

Trapattoni stepped down as coach after twenty-one games (7 wins, 3 draws, 11 losses, goals 18–33, 24 points) before he was dismissed. He resigned during the Cup quarter-finals, which Cagliari lost 1–0, 2–4 against Atalanta Bergamo.

1996/97, BAYERN MUNICH

Bundesliga winner; out of the Cup in the quarter-finals, 0–1 against Karlsruher SC. Winner of the League Cup, 2–0 against Stuttgart. Eliminated in the first round of the UEFA Cup, 0–3, 1–0 against Valencia.

1997/98, BAYERN MUNICH

Bundesliga, second place; Cup winners on 16 May 1998 in Berlin, 2–1 against MSV Duisburg. Trapattoni celebrated his biggest win as coach in the first Cup round with a 16–1 away win against DJK Waldberg. Eliminated in the quarter-finals of the Champions League, 0–0, 0–1 after extra time against Borussia Dortmund, coached by fellow countryman Nevio Scala.

1998/99, FIORENTINA

League, third place; runners-up in the Cup, 1–1, 2–2 against Parma. Eliminated in the second round of the UEFA Cup, against Grasshoppers Zürich, due to disqualification.

1999/2000, FIORENTINA

League, seventh place; out of the Cup in the second round, 0–0,

1–1 against Venezia. Eliminated in the second group stage of the Champions League.

2004/05, BENFICA LISBON

Super Liga winner; runners-up in the Cup, 1–2 on 29 May 2005 against Vitória Setúbal. Failed to qualify for the Champions League, lost in third round of the UEFA Cup, 0–2, 1–1 against CSKA Moscow.

2005/06, VFB STUTTGART

After twenty games in charge (5 wins, 12 draws, 3 losses, goals 22–18, 27 points), Trapattoni was fired; out of the Cup in the second round, 2–3 against Hansa Rostock. Eliminated in the third round of the UEFA Cup, 1–2, 1–0 against Middles-brough.

2006/07, RED BULL SALZBURG

Won the national championship. Eliminated in Champions League qualification, 1–0, 0–3 against Valencia; eliminated in the first round of the UEFA Cup, 2–2, 0–2 against Blackburn Rovers.

2007/08, RED BULL SALZBURG

Runners-up in the League. Lost in the Champions League qualifying round against Donezk, 1–0, 1–3, and in the first round of the UEFA Cup against AEK Athens, 0–3, 1–0.

SQUAD DETAILS FOR LEAGUE TEAMS

1976/77, JUVENTUS

Zoff (30 games); Cuccureddu (29), Gentile (29); Furino (26), Morini (26), Scirea (30); Causio (30), Tardelli (28), Boninsegna (29), Benetti (30), Bettega (30); Cabrini (7), Gori (7), Spinosi (7), Marchetti (6).

1977/78, JUVENTUS

Zoff (30); Cuccureddu (30), Gentile (28); Furino (26), Morini (26), Scirea (29); Causio (30), Tardelli (26), Boninsegna (21), Benetti (27), Bettega (30); Cabrini (15), Fanna (13), Virdis (10), Spinosi (5), Verza (5).

1980/81, JUVENTUS
Zoff (30); Cuccureddu (29), Cabrini (28); Furino (24), Gentile (27), Scirea (29); Causio (25), Tardelli (28), Bettega (25), Brady (28), Fanna (29); Marocchino (24), Prandelli (20), Verza (14), Osti (6), Brio (4), Galderisi (1), Storgato (1).

1981/82, JUVENTUS
Zoff (30); Gentile (27), Cabrini (29), Furino (27), Brio (29), Scirea (30); Marocchino (29), Tardelli (22), Galderisi (16), Brady (29), Virdis (30); Bonini (28), Fanna (21), Prandelli (8), Bettega (7), Osti (6), Rossi (3), Tavola (3).

1983/84, JUVENTUS
Tacconi S. (23); Gentile (24), Cabrini (29), Bonini (29), Brio (26), Scirea (30); Penzo (25), Tardelli (28), Rossi P. (30), Platini (28), Boniek (27); Vignola (25), Caricola II (20), Prandelli (17), Bodini (7), Tavola (2), Furino (1), Koetting (1).

1985/86, JUVENTUS
Tacconi S. (30); Favero (30), Cabrini (30), Bonini (26), Brio (29), Scirea (25); Mauro II (28), Manfredonia (23), Serena (25), Platini (30), Laudrup (29); Pin G. (21), Pioli (14), Pacione (12), Briaschi (10), Caricola (5), Bonetti (2).

1988/89, INTER MILAN
Zenga (33); Bergomi (32), Brehme (31); Matteoli (32), Ferri (31), Mandorlini (26); Bianchi (31), Berti (32), Diaz (33), Matthäus (32), Serena (32); Baresi (32), Verdelli (20), Fanna (13), Morello (10), Galvani (3), Malgioglio (1), Rivolta (1), Rocco (1).

1996/97, BAYERN MUNICH
Kahn (32), Scheuer (2), Babbel (31), Basler (27), Gerster (3), Hamann (23), Helmer (24), Jancker (22), Klinsmann (33), Kreuzer (9), Kuffour (22), Lakies (1), Matthäus (28), Münch (11), Nerlinger (32), Rizzitelli (25), Scholl (23), Strunz (19), Witeczek (28), Zickler (33), Ziege (27).

2004/05, BENFICA
Quim (19), Moreira (15), Luisao (29), Rocha (25), Miguel (22), Manuel dos Santos (21), Fyssas (16), Argel (10), Amoreirinha (8),

Alcides (6), André Luís (1), Geovanni (31), Manuel Fernandes (29), Petit (29), Pereira (27), Aguiar (19), Nuno Assis (15), Zlatko Zahovic (10), Almeida (6), Everson (1), Simao (34), Karadas (27), Gomez (23), Mantorras (15), Sokota (11), Carlitos (10), Delibasíc (3).

2006/07, RED BULL SALZBURG

Ochs (34), Özcan (2), Dudic (30), Linke (27), Vargas (26), Meyer (24), Bodnár (19), Steinhöfer (16), Miyamoto (9), Winklhofer (7), Orosz (5), Pichorner (1), Carboni (33), Aufhauser (30), Jezek (29), N. Kovac (28), Piták (26), Janocko (18), Tiffert (18), Alex (9), Kirchler (4), Ivanschitz (1), Vonlanthen (35), Zickler (29), Lokvenc (23), Janko (8), Vujic (1).

TEAM DETAILS FOR EUROPEAN FINALS

UEFA CUP, 1976/1977

FIRST LEG

Stadio Comunale, Turin, 4 May 1977

Spectators: 75,000

Juventus–Athletic Bilbao: 1–0 (1–0)

Goal: Tardelli (15')

Juventus: Zoff; Cuccereddu, Gentile, Scirea, Morini; Tardelli, Furino, Benetti; Causio, Boninsegna (Gori), Bettega.

Athletic Bilbao: Iribar; Oñaederra, Escalza, Guoicoechea, Guisasola; Villa, Irureta, José Angelo Rojo, Churruca; Dani, José Francisco Rojo.

SECOND LEG

San Mames Stadium, Bilbao, 18 May 1977

Spectators: 43,000

Athletic Bilbao–Juventus: 2–1 (1–1)

Goals: 0–1 Bettega (7'), 1–1 Churruca (11'), 2–1 Carlos (78')

Athletic Bilbao: Iribar, Lasa (Carlos), Guisasola, Alesanco, Escalza, Villa, Churruca, Irureta, Amarrortu, Dani, José Francisco Rojo.

Juventus: Zoff; Cuccureddu, Morini, Scirea, Gentile, Causio, Tardelli, Furino, Benetti, Boninsegna (Spinosi), Bettega.

EUROPEAN CUP, 1982/83

Stadio Olympiako, Athens, 25 May 1983

Spectators: 75,000

Hamburg SV–Juventus: 1–0 (1–0)

Goal: Magath (7')

Hamburg SV: Stein, Kaltz, Hieronymus, Jakobs, Wehmeyer, Groh, Rolff, Magath, Milewski, Bastrup (Von Heesen), Hrubesch.

Juventus: Zoff, Gentile, Brio, Scirea, Cabrini, Bonini, Tardelli, Bettega, Platini, Rossi (Marocchino), Boniek.

CUP WINNERS' CUP, 1983/84

St Jakob, Basel, 16 May 1984

Spectators: 60,000

Juventus–FC Porto: 2–1 (2–1)

Goals: 1–0 Vignola (12'), 1–1 Sousa (29'), 2–1 Boniek (41')

Juventus: Tacconi, Gentile, Brio, Scirea, Cabrini, Tardelli, Bonini, Vignola (Caricola), Platini, Rossi, Boniek.

FC Porto: Zé Beto, João Pinto, Lima Pereira, Enrico, Eduardo Luís (Costa), Magalhaes (Walsh), Frasco, Pacheco, Sousa; Gomes, Vermelinho.

UEFA SUPER CUP, 1984

Stadio Comunale, Turin, 16 January 1985

Spectators: 55,384

Juventus–Liverpool: 2–0 (1–0)

Goals: 1–0 Boniek (39'), 2–0 Boniek (79')

Juventus: Bodini; Favero, Cabrini, Brio, Scirea; Bonini, Platini, Tardelli; Briaschi, Rossi, Boniek

Liverpool: Grobbelaar; Neal, Kennedy, Lawrenson (Gillespie), Hansen; Nicol, MacDonald, Whelan, Wark; Rush, Walsh

EUROPEAN CUP, 1984/85

Heysel Stadium, Brussels, 29 May 1985

Spectators: 58,000

Juventus–Liverpool: 1–0 (0–0)

Goal: Platini (56', penalty)

Juventus: Tacconi; Favero, Cabrini, Brio, Scirea; Bonini, Platini, Tardelli; Briaschi (Prandelli), Rossi (Vignola), Boniek.

Liverpool: Grobbelaar; Neal, Beglin, Lawrenson (Gillespie), Hansen; Nicol, Dalglish, Whelan, Wark; Rush, Walsh (Johnson).

WORLD CLUB CUP, 1985

Tokyo, 8 December 1985

Spectators: 62,000

Juventus–Argentinas Juniors: 2–2 (0–0, 0–0) AET

Goals: 0–1 Ereros (55'), 1–1 Platini (63', penalty), 1–2 Castro (75'), 2–2 Laudrup (82')

Juventus won 4–2 on penalties.

Juventus: Tacconi; Favero, Cabrini, Bonini, Brio, Scirea (64' Pioli), Mauro (78', Briaschi), Manfredonia, Serena, Platini, Laudrup

Argentinas Juniors: Vidallé; Pavoni, Domenech, Villaba; Batista, Olguín, Castro, Videla; Borghi, Commisso (82', Renato Corsi), Ereros (117', López).

UEFA CUP, 1990/91

FIRST LEG

San Siro Stadium, Milan, 8 May 1991

Spectators: 68,887

Inter Milan–AS Roma: 2–0 (0–0)

Goals: 1–0 Matthäus (55', penalty), 2–0 Berti (67')

Inter Milan: Zenga; Bergomi, Brehme, Battistini, Ferri; Paganin (65', Baresi), Bianchi, Berti, Matthäus; Klinsmann, Serena (90', Pizzi)

AS Roma: Cervone; Tempestilli, Nela, Berthold, Aldair (72', Carboni), Comi (75', Muzzi); Gerolin, Di Mauro, Giannini; Völler, Rizzitelli

SECOND LEG

Stadio Olimpico, Rome, 22 May 1991

Spectators: 70,901

AS Roma–Inter: 1–0 (0–0)

Goal: Rizzitelli (81')

AS Roma: Cervone; Tempestilli (57', Salsano), Gerolin, Berthold, Aldair, Nela, Desideri (69', Muzzi), Di Mauro, Giannini, Völler, Rizzitelli

Inter Milan: Zenga, Bergomi, Brehme, Battistini, Ferri, Paganin, Bianchi, Berti, Matthäus, Klinsmann, Pizzi (67', Mandorlini)

UEFA CUP, 1992/93

FIRST LEG

Westfalen Stadium, Dortmund, 5 May 1993

Spectators: 37,000

Borussia Dortmund–Juventus: 1–3 (1–2)

Goals: 1–0 Rummenigge (2'), 1–1 D. Baggio (26'), 1–2 R. Baggio (31'), 1–3 R. Baggio (74')

Borussia Dortmund: Klos, Reinhardt, Franck (46', Mill), Schmidt, Grauer, Lusch, Reuter, Zorc (70', Karl), Chapuisat, Rummenigge, Poschner

Juventus: Peruzzi, Carrera, De Marchi, D. Baggio, Kohler, Júlio

190

César, Conte, Marocchi, Vialli, R. Baggio (76', Di Canio), Möller (88', Galia)

SECOND LEG

Stadio Delle Alpi, Turin, 19 May 1993

Spectators: 62,781

Juventus–Borussia Dortmund: 3–0 (2–0)

Goals: 1–0 D. Baggio (5'), 2–0 D. Baggio (43'), 3–0 Möller (65')

Juventus: Peruzzi, Carrera, Torricelli (66', Di Canio), De Marchi, Kohler, Júlio César, Galia, D.Baggio, Vialli (80', Ravanelli), R.Baggio, Möller

Borussia Dortmund: Klos, Reinhardt, Schmidt, Schulz, Zelic, Paschner, Reuter (65', Lusch), Karl, Sippel, Rummenigge (44', Franck), Mill

COACHES WITH THE MOST GAMES IN EUROPEAN CUP COMPETITIONS (INCLUDING THE UEFA CUP), AS OF MAY 2008

Sir Alex Ferguson 214 (1981–2008)

Giovanni Trapattoni 200 (1975–2008)

Arsene Wenger 154 (1988–2008)

RECORD AS ITALIAN NATIONAL TEAM COACH

Total: 44 games, 25 wins, 12 draws, 7 losses, goals 68–30

	DATE	PLACE	OPPONENT	RESULT
1	3.09.00	Budapest	Hungary	2–2
2	7.10.00	Milan	Romania	3–0
3	11.10.00	Ancona	Georgia	2–0
4	15.11.00	Turin	England	1–0
5	28.02.01	Rome	Argentina	1–2
6	24.03.01	Bucharest	Romania	2–0
7	28.03.01	Trieste	Lithuania	4–0
8	25.04.01	Perugia	South Africa	1–0
9	2.06.01	Tiblis	Georgia	2–1

10	1.09.01	Kaunas	Lithuania	0–0
11	5.09.01	Piacenza	Morocco	1–0
12	6.10.01	Parma	Hungary	1–0
13	7.11.01	Saitama	Japan	1–1
14	13.02.02	Catania	USA	1–0
15	27.03.02	Leeds	England	2–1
16	17.04.02	Milan	Uruguay	1–1
17	18.05.02	Prague	Czech Republic	0–1
18	3.06.02	Sapporo	Ecuador	2–0
19	8.06.02	Ibaraki	Croatia	1–2
20	14.06.02	Oita	Mexico	1–1
21	18.06.02	Daejeon	South Korea	1–2
22	21.08.02	Trieste	Slovenia	0–1
23	7.09.02	Baku	Azerbaijan	2–0
24	12.10.02	Naples	Serbia-Montenegro	1–1
25	16.10.02	Cardiff	Wales	1–2
26	20.11.02	Turkey	Pescara	1–1
27	12.02.03	Genoa	Portugal	1–0
28	29.03.03	Palermo	Finland	2–0
29	30.04.03	Genf	Switzerland	2–1
30	4.06.03	Campobasso	Northern Ireland	2–0
31	11.06.03	Helsinki	Finland	2–0
32	20.08.03	Stuttgart	Germany	1–0
33	6.09.03	Milan	Wales	4–0
34	10.09.03	Belgrade	Serbia-Montenegro	1–1
35	11.10.03	Reggio Calabria	Azerbaijan	4–0
36	12.11.03	Warsaw	Poland	1–3
37	16.11.03	Ancona	Romania	1–0
38	18.02.04	Palermo	Czech Republic	2–2
39	31.03.04	Braga	Portugal	2–1
40	28.04.04	Genoa	Spain	1–1
41	30.05.04	Tunis	Tunisia	4–0
42	14.06.04	Guimaraes	Denmark	0–0
43	18.06.04	Porto	Sweden	1–1
44	22.06.04	Guimaraes	Bulgaria	2–1